Collector's Guide to Vintage Tablecloths

Pamela Glasell
Photography by Pearl Yeadon
and Glenn L. Glasell

Schiffer Publishing Ltd

4880 Lower Valley Road, Atglen, PA 19310 USA

Acknowledgments

I have many people to thank for assisting me in the preparation of this book. Special thanks to Ted Matthews of Springs Industries, Inc., for providing me with the detailed history of the company and patiently answering all my questions. The William Elliott White Homestead organization, especially Ann Evans and the White family, for assisting me with my research into the Springmaid organization. Extra big thanks to Toni Caubel, of WestPoint Stevens Inc., for allowing my collection of colorful vintage Simtex advertisements to be used in the book.

My mother, Pearl Yeadon Erny, for showing her true photographic talents in the fabulous scenic tablecloth pictures for the book. My husband, Glenn, who came home each night to faithfully photograph four hundred tablecloths. My aunt and uncle, Richard and Marith Willis, for allowing us to use their incredible Pennsylvania gardens for our outdoor shots, and assisting with editing of the book. Mary Roell, who lent us the beautiful Victorian black hat. Martha Gaska for the lovely champagne scene. *Zeiggler's in The Country Antiques* in Hershey, Pennsylvania for letting us photograph in their gardens. My best friends, Sonja and Don Gibson, for opening up their Southern California hilltop estate for wonderful scenic pictures and providing me support in every way. And for Don's father, Errol Gibson, whose guiding spirit was with us while we were taking great pictures with his camera.

Copyright © 2002 by Pamela Glasell
Library of Congress Control Number: 2002101777

All rights reserved. No part of this work may be reproduced or used in any form or by any means—graphic, electronic, or mechanical, including photocopying or information storage and retrieval systems—without written permission from the copyright holder.
"Schiffer," "Schiffer Publishing Ltd. & Design," and the "Design of pen and ink well" are registered trademarks of Schiffer Publishing Ltd.

Designed by "Sue"
Type set in Van Dijk/ZapfHumanist BT

ISBN: 0-7643-1616-8
Printed in China
1 2 3 4

Published by Schiffer Publishing Ltd.
4880 Lower Valley Road
Atglen, PA 19310
Phone: (610) 593-1777; Fax: (610) 593-2002
E-mail: Schifferbk@aol.com
Please visit our web site catalog at
www.schifferbooks.com
We are always looking for people to write books on new and related subjects. If you have an idea for a book, please contact us at the above address.

This book may be purchased from the publisher.
Include $3.95 for shipping.
Please try your bookstore first.
You may write for a free catalog.

In Europe, Schiffer books are distributed by
Bushwood Books
6 Marksbury Avenue
Kew Gardens
Surrey TW9 4JF England
Phone: 44 (0) 20 8392 8585
Fax: 44 (0) 20 8392 9876
E-mail: Bushwd@aol.com
Free postage in the UK. Europe: air mail at cost.

Dedication

For my grandparents, Dr. Ralph Y. McGinnis, who showed me the power and beauty of the written word, and Helen Betty McGinnis, who taught me the beauty and joy of antiques and crafting;

For my mother, Dr. Pearl Yeadon Erny, who gave me the gift of music, supported me in every way, and showed me that beautiful photographs can sing;

For my husband, Glenn, for his love and encouragement. And of course, for my children, Matthew and Michelle, whose love is my greatest treasure.

Contents

Introduction 4
Chapter 1. History of American Household Textiles 5
Chapter 2. Victorian: 1840 - 1899 7
Chapter 3. Art Nouveau: 1900 14
Chapter 4. World War I: 1910s 18
Chapter 5. Art Deco: 1920s 22
Chapter 6. The Depression: 1930s 28
Chapter 7. World War II: 1940s 46
Chapter 8. Prosperity: 1950s 95
Chapter 9. Dating tablecloths 141
    Overview 142
    History of Dyes 142
    Trademark History 145
    Mandatory Content and Performance Labels 145
    Types of Printing Processes 145
    Quick Reference Summary 149
Chapter 10. Future Collectibles 150
    Designer Signed Tablecloths 151
    Themed Tablecloths 153
    Sentimental Tablecloths 153
Chapter 11. Reproductions 154
Chapter 12. Stain Removal Guide 158
    General Guidelines 159
    Definitions 161
    Out Darn Spot! 161
Chapter 13. Care and Storage of Vintage Linens 163
    Displaying Your Treasures 164
    Restoring "Mint with Tag" Vintage Linens 164
Chapter 14. Creative Crafts 165
Chapter 15. Tablecloth Manufacturers and Their Product Lines 170
Chapter 16. Useful Resources 174
Glossary 176
Bibliography 176

Introduction

*I have no yesterdays, Time took them away.
Tomorrow may not be, but I have today.*
—Pearl Yeadon McGinnis

OK, I admit it, I am obsessed. It started innocently enough with two old printed tablecloths of my grandmother's that I inherited several years ago. They were bright red strawberry patterned cloths, classic 1940s. They immediately brought back memories of my Grandmother Helen Betty McGinnis. Her kitchen, was a warm happy place full of love, kisses, and cinnamon toast. As a little girl visiting her in the summer, I would help set the tables for her ladies' bridge parties. She would let me choose tablecloths from her collection of vivid fruits, charming florals, and wonderful geometric prints. When I was finished decorating, the living room was filled with lavish colors and charming designs.

After I received those two vintage tablecloths, I simply had to have more. I was hooked. When I put one on my table, I was lost in the beautiful designs of days gone by, transported back to a simpler time, when I didn't have to check my email, pay my cable bill, or coordinate my children's play dates. I began searching every antique store and flea market in Southern California, and had my wonderful mother buy every tablecloth in Southwest Missouri until I had a collection that numbered well over four hundred. Every time I brought another treasure home my sweet husband would remark, "Don't you already have enough tablecloths?" as if *that* were possible. My darling children would ask, "Can we eat on this one mom?" So, to justify my ever-growing collection, I became a dealer in vintage linens. I now buy and sell vintage tablecloths and linens and share my love of these pieces of kitchen history with other "obsessed" collectors through my on-line store, Gramas Attic Antiques and Collectibles.

Currently the collectible vintage tablecloth market is "taking off," and prices and demand for these classic treasures have risen sharply. More and more collectors are drawn to these wonderful cloths, bringing the glorious past to their present kitchen tables. Tablecloths unify everything on the table, adding color, patterns, texture, and whimsy. With an afternoon at the local flea market and a couple of dollars, you can build an entire vintage tablecloth collection. You can change ambience and flavor from summer to winter, spring to fall, or romantic to fun. Dress your table up or down — there is no end to the fun you can have decorating with these elaborate vintage designs.

Whether it is the memories of Grandma's Sunday dinners served on her best linen damask tablecloth, or the lunch table set with a cheerful bright strawberry cloth, we are all drawn to the lovely vintage fabrics and the endless variety of dazzling patterns and designs. The romantic floral themes, resembling "just picked" blooming floral bouquets, provide an ever-growing garden of delight for our dreary winter kitchens. Vintage tablecloth collectors will agree, it's the vivid colors and whimsical designs that linger in our memories and bring smiles to our hearts.

Over two years ago, I set out to create a history of the vintage tablecloth, to discover the origins, the major manufacturers, and the evolution of dyes, fabrics, and designs. This has been an on-going and sometimes extremely challenging process of discovery. The search for information from the few sources that were available on vintage fabrics, kitchen textiles, and other related printed cotton manufacturing sources gave me the foundation for this collector's guide. I wanted to give vintage tablecloth collectors a reference book that would contain information for accurately dating their collection, providing interesting details about some of the major manufacturers, and of course, show pictures of hundreds of wonderful vintage tablecloths. A visual feast for the eyes and soul.

The values in the price guide section were taken from a variety of sources, including on-line auction sites, vintage linen collectors, and antique dealers. The values assigned for the tablecloths shown are in a range of "good condition" to "mint." If the tablecloth you have is significantly damaged, subtract 25% from the lowest value given; if it is "mint with the tag," add 25% to the highest value given for a more accurate value.

Writing this book has been an exciting journey for me, a chance to expand my knowledge and to rediscover the history of days gone by. My tablecloth collection now has a value that goes far beyond its monetary one. Each cloth has both a sentimental and emotional value, its own rich history that I am happy to share with you. So pull out your favorite vintage tablecloth and pour a fragrant cup of tea. This book was written for you, my fellow obsessed tablecloth collector and friend. Enjoy!

—Pamela Glasell

Chapter 1
History of American Household Textiles

Tablecloths have played a rich part in the daily lives and family traditions of Americans, and for most of us, are associated with wonderful memories of family and celebrations. They have enjoyed a long and colorful history in America; in Colonial times, for example, they were so valuable that they were itemized and handed down in wills. Their progression from tablecloth to kitchen rag was even carefully documented in household diaries and inventories.

During the period between the 1600s and the end of the eighteenth century, Americans produced a significant number of textiles used for household furnishings but were still dependent on imported materials from Europe, which was the dominant industrial power of the time. Simple homespun fabrics, pieces of heirloom lace, heavy tapestry rugs, and coarse linen all graced the early settlers' wooden tables. During colonial times, it was proper to have a tablecloth or rug on the table until the main course, when it was removed and the rest of the meal was then eaten on the bare wood tabletop. In upper class homes, the removing of the cloth was an elaborate ceremony in itself. It was a difficult task, requiring four footmen at each side of the table while two more servants held the heavy centerpiece. The cloth was then gathered up and removed by the butler.

Americans who lived in seaport towns and cities were the major recipients of imported European goods. The large majority of Americans who lived in rural villages had to grow and produce their own materials, like the cottons, linens, and flax that were needed to make cloth. During this period there were a small number of men who were proficient weavers. Their job was to make cloth from the natural materials grown by the colonists. These skilled weavers plied their trade in every colony. Some maintained shops of their own; others packed up their looms and traveled the countryside.

America's access to good quality cloth was limited until the New England mills began weaving an adequate supply of American-made fabric in the early 1800s. This was largely due to the invention of cotton processing machines, which revolutionized the industry in the United States. The most important of these was invented in 1794 by a reclusive schoolmaster who taught the children of a cotton plantation in the south. Eli Whitney was present on many occasions when southern plantation owners complained that it took twenty slaves a whole day to pick and clean twenty pounds of cotton. It was time consuming, tedious work to clean the cotton of the seeds. Eli was intrigued by the problem and, in his spare time, came up with a box with a suspended cylinder that revolved and shed the seeds. This simple invention revolutionized the south and catapulted the American textile mills into their golden age.

In 1790, Samuel Slater, a British mechanic, developed the first successful American cotton-spinning mill in Pawtucket, Rhode Island. Slater Mills began producing textiles for yard goods and table linens. In 1835, in Boston, Massachusetts, Indian Head Mills began producing cotton "gray goods." This is material just as it leaves the loom but before it is given any finishing treatment and is usually "gray" in color. The cotton mill industry thrived in the South between 1850 and 1860, but production was only small-scale to meet the local needs of an agrarian society. After 1860, new mills were being built and were prospering in the three states that would eventually dominate the southern textile Industry: North Carolina, South Carolina, and Georgia.

Mills were so important that towns sprang up around them, becoming self-contained little communities that provided every need for the mill employees. Startex, South Carolina, is a good example of this; even after the mill closed in 2000, the town still retained its benefactor's name. People in mill towns like Startex had always been the most dependent on their mills, which historically were the employers of the majority of the townspeople. The mill owned everything — houses, schools, the post office — and was the source of city services like water, power, and sewer. The mills were equally dependent on the local townspeople to run their business. Entire generations of families worked at the mill, engraining themselves in the history and culture of the mill communities.

Another important textile manufacturer of today had a remarkable early beginning. Springs Industries was founded as Fort Mills Manufacturing Company in Fort Mill, South Carolina in 1887. The founder, Samuel Elliott White (1837-1911), was a colorful, brilliant pioneer of early cotton textile mills in the South. His son, Colonel Leroy Springs (1861-1931), President of the six cotton mills that would become the Springmaid company, was an equally charismatic leader. He felt so close to his company and to his people, that when he died in 1931 he was buried on the front lawn of the Lancaster Cotton Mills plant no.3.

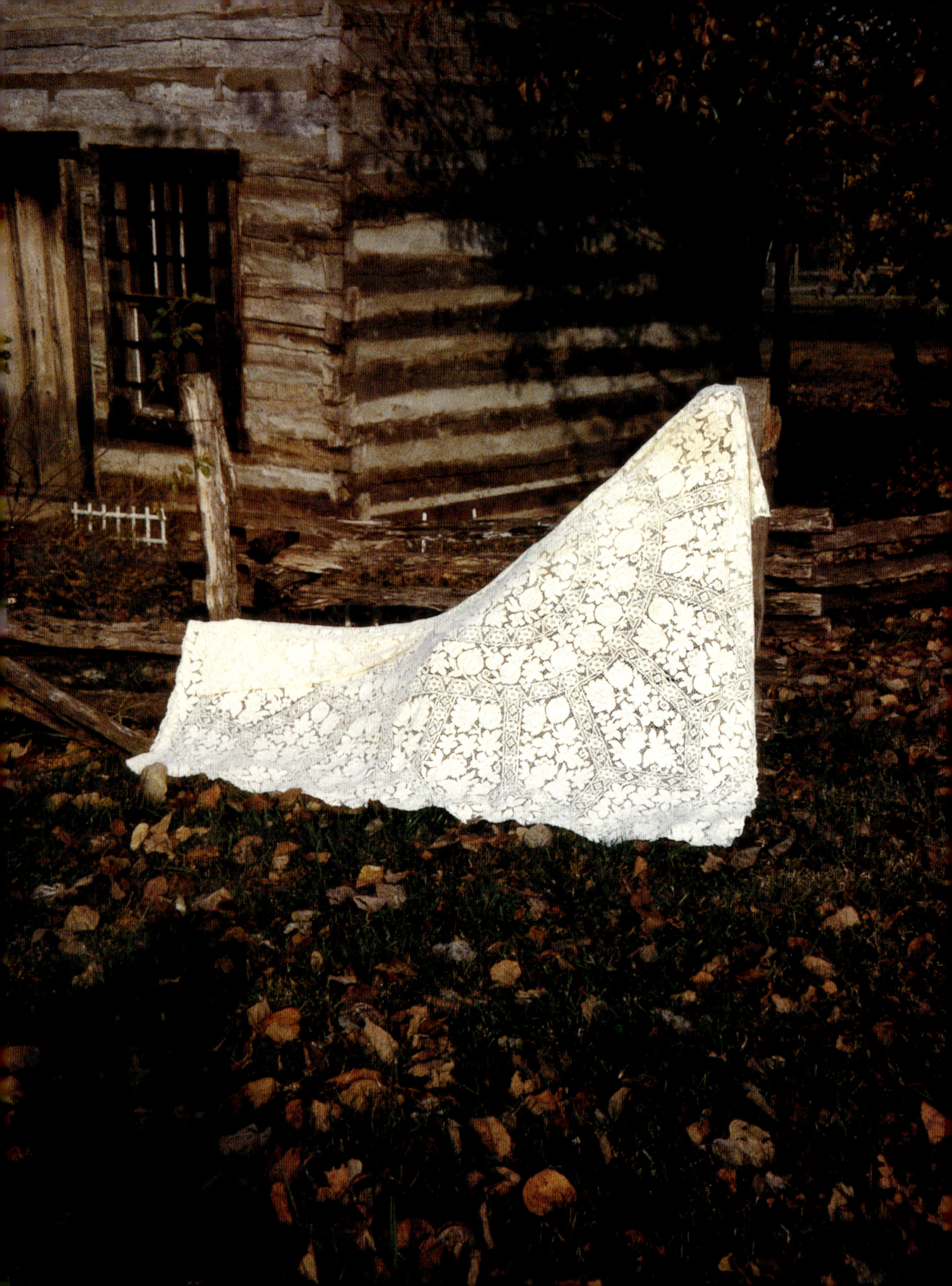

Chapter 2
Victorian: 1840-1899

In the thirty-five years between the Civil War and the end of the nineteenth century (1865-1899), America was in the midst of widespread industrialization. Electric lights, the sewing machine, the telephone, and the camera were just some of the things that were invented during this time. These new inventions not only revolutionized the American textile manufacturing industry but also lightened the load of the average housewife, allowing her more freedom and encouraging artistic endeavors that can be seen in the incredibly detailed embroidery and lacework on tablecloths that came from this era.

In the United States, this period also marked the beginning of a long period of immigration from central and Eastern Europe, providing the labor essential to the growth of the American textile industry and fueling the "industrial revolution" in America. During most of the late 1800s, Queen Victoria, who had lost her beloved Prince Albert, made it fashionable to be a widow. This influence produced the dark, somber, and opulent Victorian colors and styles that characterize the textile fabrics from 1850-1900. The Victorian's love of rich deep textures, elaborately woven tapestries, fringed table toppers, and woven tablecloths is well known, and the Victorians used these to cover everything. The invention of the parlor lamp gave the Victorians yet another reason to buy a tapestry or make a table cover for use under the lamp. The Industrial Revolution had provided the majority of the urban population new prosperity and wealth, and they were eager to show off with their lavish furnishings and rich table linens.

Early textile mills were located along rivers on the East Coast and in North and South Carolina. Cannon Mills of Concord, North Carolina, one of the most profitable mills of this time, was founded in 1875 by J. W. Cannon and sold early table linens under their "Table Queen" label. John P. Stephens, founder of J.P. Stevens & Co., has a rich family history that goes back to the war of 1812. His grandfather, Nathaniel Stevens, started in the textile business in 1812. Nathaniel's son Moses, John's uncle, took over the textile company and made it one of the largest in the country. John P. (J.P.) Stevens started his career working for a Boston dry-goods commission house, Faulkner Page & Co., and by 1899 he had enough money to establish his own dry-goods commission house in New York City, named J.P. Stevens & Co. His commission house prospered by selling the products of his uncle's textile company. J.P. Stevens also purchased interests in many textile firms in New England and was one of the first textile industrialists to invest heavily in mills in the South. Stevens purchased the "Simtex" and "Rosemary" companies in the late 1960s. In 1988, J.P. Stevens merged with another of the oldest textile manufacturing companies, WestPoint Manufacturing Company, established in 1873.

The abundance of goods produced in the late 1800s led to the establishment of the large chain department store. Many upscale department stores were created during this time, including Bloomingdale's in 1872, R. H. Macys in 1874, and Sears Roebuck and Company in 1893. Quantity buying from local American manufacturers, low taxes, and cheap labor created enormous profits for these retail giants. The department stores placed fixed prices on items and encouraged "shopping." This was the new concept of strolling through the store to examine goods without prior intentions to buy. Store windows were "dressed" artistically and their lavish interiors, fashionable tearooms, and seasonal events made these stores as popular as fairs and museums. Department stores sought to create the standard of what was stylish and appropriate and to influence shoppers' needs and values.

One of the pioneers of the "department store" concept was Fuller Callaway (1870-1928). Starting at the tender age of fourteen, he broke away from conventional methods of doing business as a merchant. Callaway focused on stocking a large quantity of one item, which he could buy and sell more cheaply than the typical merchant. He also invested in and trained aggressive sales and advertising departments, the first of their kind. Around 1890, he established a full scale department store featuring a wide selection of merchandise and low prices — this all by the age of twenty. By 1915, he had invested personally in seven textile mills. His sons, Cason and Fuller Callaway Jr., eventually assumed leadership of the mills. In 1932, they consolidated the mills into Callaway Mills, which created beautiful tablecloths and other household linens.

In 1895, Sears, Roebuck and Company established a large and impressive mail order catalogue. It was such a sensation that others soon followed. Even the rural community's taste and purchases could now be influenced by department store fashions and the definition of what was "in style" and in "good taste" for the modern Victorian home. *Godey's Lady's Book*, one of the first monthly ladies' fashion magazines, was established in 1830. It could be found on every Victorian table by 1840 and contained color plates and articles on the latest fashions, proper etiquette, trends from exotic locales like Paris and England, and articles on fancy needlework and other hand crafted projects. Other publications soon followed, including *Delineator Magazine* and *Harper's Bazaar*.

Godeys Ladies Book hand tinted wood block engraving, 1850s.

Godeys Ladies Book hand tinted wood block engraving, 1850s.

Prior to the middle of the nineteenth century, all dyes were natural, obtained from various sources found in nature such as plants, coal tar, and insects. The whole process was both costly and impractical. Dyes could not be made in large quantities reliably and they had to be shipped over large distances from Turkey or the British West Indies to Europe or America. The most common and valuable dyes were: madder, a red mauve; indigo, a deep blue; and saffron yellow. These three dyes were difficult to produce and expensive. Mordant was used to help seal the color into the fabric and prevent fading.

This dye problem was solved in Turkey, where they had developed a brilliant, true, colorfast red for use in Turkish carpets. This color, known as "Turkey Red," was extremely durable and could even be laundered with great success. In 1863, William Perkins created the first commercial synthetic dye that he called "mauve." By the late 1890s, Turkey Red table linens and show towels, which were fancy linen damask towels usually with fringe that were laid across the mantle or china cabinet, were in use. You could also find mauve single color printed table covers such as the one shown here. They were offered in almost all mail order catalogs and department stores and found in every fashionable Victorian home.

From the *White House Cookbook*, 1897. Note the rich, Turkey Red fringed damask.

8 Victorian: 1840-1899

Rare, mint condition Victorian felted table cover. One color mauve stamped, unhemmed. Produced by Lladnek Canton Draperies, circa 1880s. $350.

Lladnek Canton Draperies table cover tag.

Victorian: 1840-1899   9

Table linens of this period were dark heavy tapestries, fringed Turkey Red and white damask cloths, and heavily decorated plush and velvet table toppers. Most elaborate tapestry table covers were still imported from China and Europe, but a few American textile mills were producing the rich damasks that found their way into Victorian parlors and dining rooms. Soon the dark somber crimsons, browns, and gold found in Victorian table linens were succeeded by the less dramatic but more spirited bright color schemes made possible by the creation of new chemical dyes from Germany.

By the late 1890s, such new aniline dyes had been invented in Germany, far surpassing the dull colors obtainable by vegetable dyes. They were introduced with dazzling effects, eliminating the need for the large batch dying required by the vegetable dyes. American manufacturers could now use aniline dyes, and in smaller amounts, to produce a vast array of new colors. These peacock greens, blues, magentas, violets, and raw pinks were utilized in abundance on the tablecloths of this era. Such strong colors were popular until the so-called "Aesthetic Movement" of 1899 subdued everything, and olive greens, grays, and dull blues became accepted as evidence of artistic morality and good taste.

The 1890 *American Domestic Cyclopedia* pronounced that "… every Victorian home should contain fancy table covers. The material is olive green plush with a rich border trimming with floral ribbon and fringe." A Victorian dinner table would contain "… a table covered with a thick cotton-flannel or pad under a fine linen damask. On rare occasions you can use a satin damask or handsome lace over a piece of satin." Any type of handwork, including complicated embroidery, drawn-work pieces, delicate lace, and elaborate crochet was in fashion.

The Victorians were extremely social, calling on friends every day and enjoying many occasions for social outings and dinner parties. Almost every kind of social gathering at this time was called an "at home." There were "dancing at homes," "musical at homes," and just "at homes." Strict social decorum and etiquette dictated the manners of these elaborately planned events, including what table linen to use and how far the linen should hang over the side of the table. By the end of the Victorian period, America was a hopeful nation, blessed with prosperity, excitement, and an exuberance that laid the foundation for "Ragtime Music," the "Gibson Girls," and the rush over the border to seek vast fortunes in the Klondike.

Victorian handmade bobbin lace tablecloth, circa 1890s. $250.

Hand woven jacquard tablecloth with early vegetable dyed and tufted embroidery, circa 1860s. $200-$400.

Close-up of homespun jacquard tablecloth. Note the uneven loose weave.

Victorian woven silk table cover, circa 1890. $150.

Turkey Red jacquard woven tablecloth with fringe, circa 1890. $250-$500.

Victorian: 1840-1899 11

Turkey Red sweet pea linen damask tablecloth, circa 1890. $75-$125.

A Turkey Red damask show towel. Draped over a mantle, or used on a tea tray, this was in every Victorian's home in the late 1890s. $75-$100.

Victorian Turkey Red federal eagle damask tablecloth, circa 1890s. $75-$150.

12   Victorian: 1840-1899

Victorian griffin embroidered tablecloth. Chrome yellow and black thread on homespun linen, circa 1890. $125-$150.

Close-up of Victorian griffin tablecloth. Note the delicate stitches and uneven weave of the linen.

Victorian: 1840-1899   13

Chapter 3
Art Nouveau: 1900

Victorian linen damask formal tablecloth, circa 1900. Notice how the sides are longer than a contemporary tablecloth. $125-$150.

The beginning of the twentieth century was a period of remarkable change and newfound prosperity. President McKinley was assassinated and Vice President Theodore Roosevelt was catapulted into the White House, delighting the nation with his promise to "speak softly and carry a big stick." The first trip across the United States in a gas-powered car took fifty-two days and the Wright Brothers made history with the first airplane flight in a little known grassy field.

"Art Nouveau," a new style in visual arts and architecture, was first shown at the 1900 World's Fair in Paris. Literally meaning "new art," Art Nouveau was developed by a brilliant and energetic generation of artists and designers. They sought to fashion an art form appropriate to the modern age by breaking free from the constraints of the somber Victorian age and the pressures of the Industrial Revolution. Art Nouveau designers believed that all the arts should work in harmony to create a "total work of art." Buildings, furniture, and household textiles all conformed to these principles. Tablecloths from this era have a crisp Art Nouveau styling and are characterized by geometric prints, squares, circles, stylized florals, good luck symbols, horseshoes, wishbones, laurel wreaths, and ribbon and animal prints. Art Nouveau fashion brought flat, pastel colors: silver gray, pale greens, and blues, muted Turkey Reds, dim orange, pink, mauve, and violet. They must have seemed fresh and charming to the Victorians, so long accustomed to the stodgy, gloomy dark colors of the earlier Victorian age.

The Montgomery Ward Catalogue from 1902 shows Turkey Red and Turkey Red and green combination woven jacquard tablecloths with fringe, as well as boxed sets of linen damasks in red, yellow, gold, and salmon. Tapestry and velvet plush table covers were also featured, with or without fringe, for the parlor table. "Table squares" of small pieces of bleached white damask with white designs were also featured in various sizes: 18", 24", 32", and 36". The etiquette of the time stated that the tablecloth should hang down a quarter of a yard over the edge of the table. You will find most tablecloths from this era are usually as wide as they were long, and will come in sizes 72" square, 64" square, or even 72" x 108". The small, colorful printed tablecloths were not fashionable for the larger dinner table at this time. They were reserved for the intimate luncheon or for breakfast tables. This fashion was in place until the 1930s when the sides of the tablecloth were shortened to 52" and 58" and it became fashionable to use a larger colorful printed tablecloth on the family dinner table.

Harper's Bazar Magazine, January 23, 1897.
From the collection of Sonja Gibson.

The 1900s rural woman continued to work almost nonstop to prepare meals, slaving over a hot stove fueled by wood, coal, or petroleum. If a woman was fortunate enough to have a cook and housekeeper, she could also take an active part in activities outside the home. Theme parties and ladies' luncheons became popular ways to socialize. It is interesting to note that most restaurants segregated their rooms by sex and/or race at this time. Elaborate dinner parties among the affluent were popular, featuring from twelve to eighteen courses made possible by full-time cooks, maids, and hired waiters, who were taken from within the ever increasing immigrant population.

Art Nouveau: 1900 15

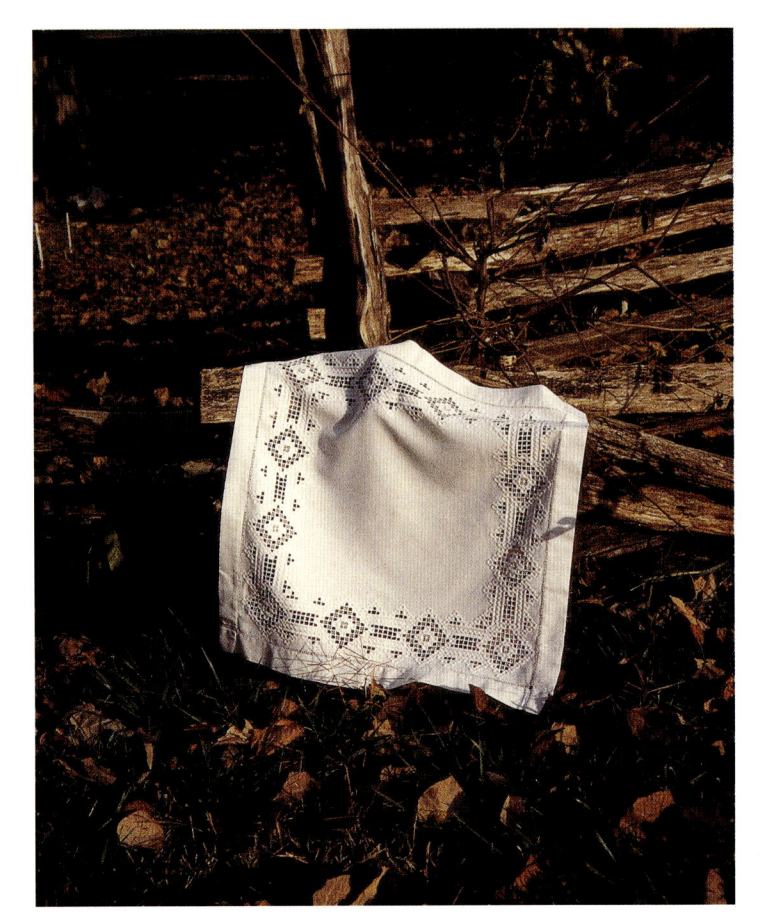

Crisp, cut work table square, circa 1900. $75-$95.

Early linen tablecloth with delicate bobbin lace mesh edges, circa 1900. $175-$300.

Yellow bordered linen damask tablecloth, crisp and elegant, circa 1900. $50-$75.

Turkey Red jacquard woven tablecloth, circa 1900. $175-$300.

Linen tablecloth one color, Art Nouveau design, 1910. $75-$100.

Delicate hand made bobbin lace tablecloth, a family heirloom, circa 1900. $325-$500.

Art Nouveau: 1900 17

Chapter 4
World War I: 1910s

Early fringed linen damask with pale blue border, most likely an import, circa 1910. $50-$75.

The United States entered 1910 as a rapidly emerging industrial giant. The newly affordable Model T rolled off the assembly line and waves of immigrants continued to pour in from Europe. This decade also saw the first transcontinental airplane flight, cross-country telephone service, and more miles of railroad track than would ever again exist in the U.S. It was a prosperous early beginning to a decade that would later find the country embroiled in a world war.

By 1914, Germany was producing about 85% of the world's supply of dyes and dyestuffs, and its trading partners were responsible for the remaining. Only seven firms in America were producing dyestuffs during this time. The war in Europe, therefore, suddenly created a huge problem for American tablecloth manufacturers. The Allied blockade of German shipping caused a "dye famine" in the U.S., forcing American textile research facilities to rush to create new sources of dyestuffs. By 1919, there were over ninety new manufacturers producing American made dyestuffs. In an attempt to deal with the dye famine, poor quality dyestuffs that had been abandoned for years were taken from warehouses and mill storerooms and used. Even colors intended for tinting of paper were sold to textile mills. These dyes were unstable and not color fast. There are very few examples of tablecloths produced between 1914 and 1920 that are still in good shape or retain their original colors.

As Americans sent their boys off to the "Great War," there was an increase in popularity of "sweetheart" printed table covers and other related textiles. Bucilla, founded in 1913, started creating stamped table linens for embroidery and, in the early 1940s, began producing lively printed tablecloths. Victory Manufacturing, founded in 1919 by Kemp and Beatley, began creating a line of colored printed damask tablecloths and by 1935 quickly became a leading producer of wonderful printed tablecloths under the names of VicRay, Victory, and KempRay. They enjoyed tremendous success as tablecloth manufacturers up until the late 1990s.

A new movement in home furnishings décor reminded people of their Colonial or early American roots and inspired a renewed interest in American history. Antique collecting became an avid pursuit; dining rooms soon filled with early American pine tables while kitchens were adorned with earthenware and Delft pottery. Styles utilizing whiplash curves, human forms with insect wings, butterflies, peacocks, women with flowing hair, the Iris flower, sensuous lines, fantasy type prints, and moon and stars were all popular themes

Home Life 1913 cover.

and could be found in the rich damask tablecloths and linen stamped, small tablecloths.

After World War I, stay-at-home wives found new interests outside the home, such as ladies' clubs, art clubs, and other social activities. Manufacturers responded with new "easy care" tablecloths. The shrinking supply of domestic servants and the availability of new electrical appliances changed household routines for many urban women. The iron and the vacuum were the most popular appliances purchased for newly electrified homes. Higher standards of cleanliness added new housekeeping burdens, and tablecloth manufacturers responded with paper labels advertising "fast colors" and promising "durable with repeated launderings." The printed colored tablecloth with more elaborate designs became more accepted and fashionable as a luncheon cloth and as a cloth for informal parties.

Simple plaid linen tablecloth, late 1910s. $25-$45.

World War I hand painted table cover, could also be used as a pillow cover. Wonderful hand painted graphics, circa 1916. $50-$75.

Linen stamped one color lunch cloth. Art Nouveau influenced design, circa 1915. $50-$75.

20　World War I: 1910s

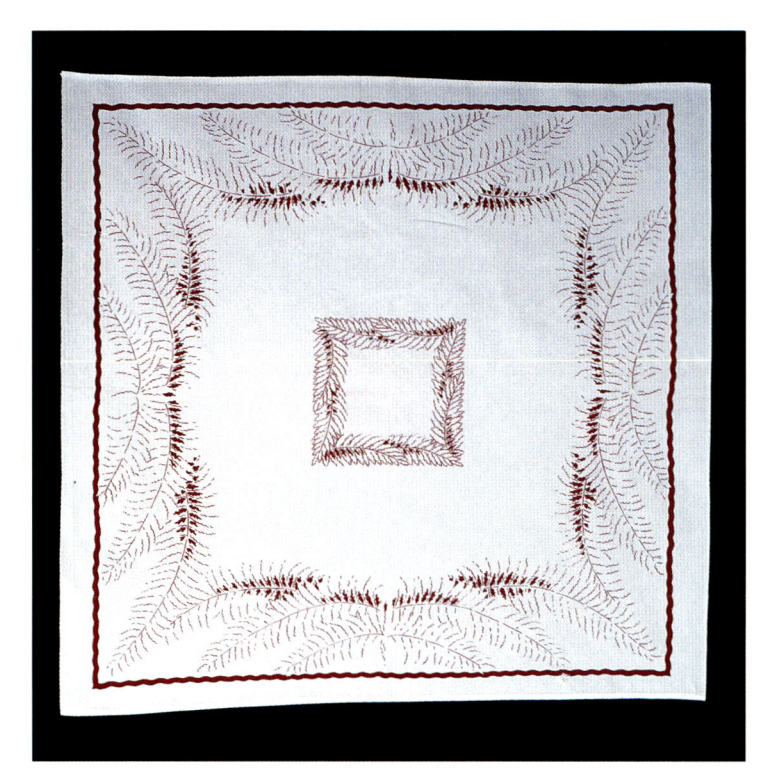

Early deep red "feathers" tablecloth. This maroon-red is indicative of the late 1910s. $50-$75.

Reverse printed, vat dyed floral tablecloth, circa 1910. $40-$55.

Colonial revival style one color stamped linen tablecloth, circa 1910. $50-$75.

World War I: 1910s 21

Chapter 5
Art Deco: 1920s

As the 1920s began, the future looked bright. This decade is often characterized as a period of American prosperity and optimism. It was the decade of the "Roaring Twenties," bathtub gin, the $5 workday, the first transatlantic flight, and the silent movie. It is also seen as a period of great social and industrial advances as the nation became urban and commercial, women won the right to vote, and the economy prospered.

President Warren G. Harding promised a "return to normalcy" after World War I and encouraged trade agreements with other countries. Czechoslovakia had become a new republic in 1918, and skilled enthusiastic artisans produced low-priced, high quality damask tablecloths. Ireland and Japan also began exporting lace and colored damask tablecloths to America. All these imported tablecloths flooded the tablecloth market. The 1922 Montgomery Wards Catalogue featured "Heavy, imported damask tablecloths and napkins to match," as well as "Best domestic table linens." These imports affected the American textile mills, not only inspiring and challenging American designers but also creating a tremendous hardship that would be felt when the Depression hit. Although sporadic tariff adjustments were made in the 1920s and 1930s, they were not enough to help and many tablecloth manufacturers shut down or left the industry.

Various social trends were at work during the 1920s. This created an era of fun and carefree lifestyles. People were spending money on electrical gadgets and appliances such as toasters, refrigerators, and gas stoves. Women had more freedom outside of the home. New models of cars were introduced almost every day, and thousands of miles of road stretched across forty-eight states. Historians have characterized the 1920s as a time of frivolity, abundance, and happy-go-lucky attitudes.

Several years had passed since the end of World War I. People felt free-spirited and wanted to have fun. As a result, kitchen textiles became less formal and more adventurous in color and style. There emerged a "carefree" influence in tablecloth design. The discovery of the treasures of King Tut's tomb in 1922 sparked an interest in the East and this became incorporated into the emerging Art Deco styles of design. "The Orient" basically meant anything in what we now call the "Third World," so styles and exotica derived from the Middle East, Asia, African, and Latin (tropical) cultures were also considered chic. Floral prints began dominating tablecloth designs, featuring the flowers and arrangements of the current gardening fads. In the 1920s, camellias, lilacs, and morning glories were some of the new flowers that were in vogue.

The 1922 Montgomery Wards Catalogue featured damask "New colored tablecloths patterned in your choice of pink, blue, or gold," which was actually a "cheddar" yellow color. They also advertised an oriental themed tablecloth: "The blue patterns are stamped by hand upon white cotton cloth of extra good quality…These inexpensive tablecloths and napkins give the table an oriental note of brightness and cheer and are much in demand for luncheon and breakfast service." The printed, two color tablecloth was now in vogue and was a "must have" for ladies' luncheons.

Rural farm communities were still thriving and were an integral part of the American culture. Large, plain cotton "feed and grain bags" used to package many types of dry seeds and grains were a big business in the early part of the twentieth century. With the diverse array of U.S. fabrics and dyes now available, the American colored printed textile sack was born. It was well known by manufacturers that the thrifty farm community recycled the used sacking (and even the string used to sew the bag) into table linens as well as other domestic textile uses. Some of the feedsacks had instructions for cutting and making tablecloth luncheon sets printed right on the sack. These sacks were of different sizes but soon the "sack" was standardized to about 1-1/3 yards of fabric. The sheer abundance of different types of fabrics and designs that we can find today is evidence that the feedbag manufacturers responded to consumer demand by enthusiastically producing many highly decorated colorful sacks. Homemade feedsack tablecloths enjoyed a tremendous popularity during this period through the late 1940s.

Softer, more pastel hues were the colors used now, though you will find that some brighter colors were also used towards the end of this period. The number of colors used to print each tablecloth increased from one to two colors by the end of the 1920s. After the mid-1920s, the red became lighter and dusty rose and other pinks were extremely popular. Some of the newly created dyes —

Miss Emily and Miss Michelle enjoying a tea party in the garden. Dutch children one color tablecloth, 1920s. $75-$100.

Sweet Dutch children, cherries, and ribbons in a one color early 1920s tablecloth. $75-$100.

Art Deco: 1920s

purples, greens, and some pinks from this era — were "fugitive," leaving a faint ghost color when they faded. True greens were still not possible to produce successfully, and for that reason gray, yellow, and even pink leaves were used in the tablecloths of this period and up until the mid 1930s.

Blues, purples, and greens were the first colors to fade. There are many tablecloths on the market today that show faint areas of missing colors while still displaying other bright colors and designs. I find the tablecloths of the 1920s and 1930s to be the most interesting: flowers that seem to be floating above their stems, pale blue or oddly colored gray fruits, and vegetables with faint outlines of other "ghost" colors giving them an almost surreal design and appeal. These are the some of the oldest printed tablecloths and have a special character of their own.

Several new factors that would affect the production of tablecloths emerged in the 1920s. Synthetic fibers like nylon, which was discovered many years earlier, began to replace cotton in tablecloths but were not fully utilized until the late 1930s. Most of the tablecloths of this early era seem to be all cotton or linen. Some tablecloth manufacturers began experimenting with linen and cotton blends for strength and durability. Eli Walker Dry Goods started selling their own line of tablecloths, "E & W" and "Brentmoore." Startex Mills and Rosemary Manufacturing were some of the textile mills that began producing tablecloths during the later part of this period.

Prohibition was in full effect by January 1920, leading to the establishment of speakeasies and elaborate cocktail parties. A majority of the cocktails that Americans drink today were created during this period when home parties, featuring alcoholic drinks and tidbits of food, were the rage. It was still polite and correct to use a white or lightly colored damask tablecloth for formal dinner parties, but with the wild home parties and dignified ladies' luncheons, bold fun prints on small lunch cloths were now in vogue.

Linen Damask advertisement, 1926.

Red, pink and white kitchen plaid tablecloth, late 1920s. $25-$35.

Unusual woven black and red tablecloth. Themes of black Americana, beer, dice, rats, and pretzels. $100-$125.

Pale mauve and gray flowing "deco" tablecloth, 1920s. $45-$55.

Art Deco: 1920s 25

Beautiful stamped "Arts and Crafts" styled tablecloth on heavy sailcloth, circa 1920s. $100-$125.

Linen stamped bold flowers, Arts and Craft style, circa 1920s. $40-$50.

Victory K&B manufactured deep pink tablecloth, intricate design of flowers and ribbons, circa 1920s. $50-$75.

26   Art Deco: 1920s

Early, two color stamped linen tablecloth, Arts and Crafts design. In mint condition it was a deeper orange and blue, but faded after one improper washing. Circa 1920s. $50-$75.

Blue discharge printed floral tablecloth, 1920s. $50-$75.

Crisp, yellow rose patterned linen damask. As offered and described in the 1922 Montgomery Wards Catalogue. $50-$75.

Art Deco: 1920s

Chapter 6

The Depression: 1930s

The early 1930s was a time of grim determination for most Americans as they struggled through the Depression. The harsh realities of daily life took a tremendous toll on the people's spirit and tested the endurance of the average American. Reckless spending was a thing of the past. The autumn 1930 Sears Catalogue admonished, "Thrift is the spirit of the day."

The newest feature of the 1930s home was the introduction of the "breakfast nook." This was a corner or side of the kitchen furnished with a small square table and four chairs, or a small table with a built-in bench. Most of the brightly printed tablecloths of the era were sized and styled to fit the kitchen's breakfast nook, where the family ate informal meals.

The beginning of the decade saw women sewing and cooking more. Home yard goods fabrics and bolts of wide kitchen fabrics were offered in department stores and by mail order catalogues for use by housewives in making their own kitchen tablecloths and aprons. Gaily printed feedsack cloths were made into tablecloths and aprons and used for other domestic and kitchen necessities.

The Chicago World's Fair in 1933 reinforced the Oriental influence on tablecloth designs. Other common themes of the 1930s were squares, wide plaids, and flower and vine prints. Garden inspired themes were popular and poppies, iris, foxgloves, dahlias, and clusters of flowers all graced mid-1930s homes. Stylized leaf and flower shapes and line drawing prints were also common. Textile Designer Marion V. Dorn (1896-1964) was extremely influential during this period with her bold print designs for rugs and tablecloths.

> The garden will become an integral part of the house. The distinction between indoors and outdoors will disappear.
> —Rudolph Schindler, Interior Designer

An interesting technique found in the 1930s is called "grinning," in which halos of white were used to separate motifs and multiple colors. This technique enabled textile printers to produce yards of fabric more quickly with less chance of an accidental overlap of colors. You can find many tablecloths where this printing technique is evident and it is a good way to date your tablecloths.

One of the distinguishing features of this time was the common use of bright, intense, multicolored prints. Pastels were not as common as in the 1920s although you will still find a few. Prints normally included color schemes composed of the opposites on the color wheel. Bright colors in contrasting combinations seemed to be the rule of the day. Blue/orange, dark green/orange, aqua with red, yellow, gold, orange and green, were often used. The prints were larger in scale, and you can find wonderful tablecloths with large distinct roses and huge bouquets of flowers gracing the corners of the tablecloths.

The "true" greens, which were not possible prior to the mid 1930s, are distinctive: Nile green, mint, or moss green were used on tablecloths of the era. But tablecloth designers still favored blue, gray, and even yellow for leaves, vines, and trees as it was probably cheaper to use these dyes. I love collecting floral tablecloths from this era with their odd gray and even blue leaves. Red and white were the norm for color accents.

Nylon was now being used in combination with other fabrics to produce an easy care tablecloth. Consumers became confused with this new fabric, which felt like silk. To assist consumers, the government required manufacturers to state on their paper labels when their products contained rayon, even in the smallest quantity.

By the mid and late 1930s, California's distinct style was made famous in large part by glamorous Hollywood movies. The 1937 *Dry Goods Economist Magazine* spotlighted a trend in "Novelty hand blocked prints interpreting typical Californian motifs…such favorites as the San Francisco Bridge, movie apparatus like megaphones and cameras." In 1937, Edith Head produced a line of fabrics called "Hollywaiian." These designs were vivid tropical florals and other adapted "Hawaiian" motifs printed on aprons, dresses, and housecoats. The line was very popular and soon influenced tablecloth manufacturers of the day. Favorite designs of the time were exaggerated and profuse, and the rich, lush, tropical "island" themes, fragrant island blooms, and elegant florals helped bring Americans out of the grim years of the Depression.

Wiel and Durrse began producing their "Wilendur" (no "e" at the end) tablecloth line in 1938. It was so successful that they added three more labels, "America's Pride," "Setting Pretty," and "Oppa-Tunity," in the early 1940s. You will find the same printed tablecloth design with all three types of tags. Leacock Prints, as well as many other manufacturers, also began producing their famous line of printed tablecloths at the end of this period. Callaway Mills was a very successful family-run textile business, printing tablecloths and other textiles from 1932 until 1960. They marked their tablecloths with a "Callaway" signature incorporated into the design. When America entered into World War II, Callaway Mills, along with other tablecloth manufacturers, temporarily stopped their tablecloth production to provide war goods for the soldiers.

The 1930s home was a place of refuge. Cooking became a respectable, even fashionable pastime among middle-class and upper class women who had been forced to let their cooks and servants go during the Depression. Women's club lunches, afternoon teas, church socials, and county fairs were all popular ways to socialize in the 1930s using gaily-printed small tablecloths. Parties with refreshments rather than meals were another important way to socialize. These events gave hostesses a chance to be creative with food and in their use of coordinating tablecloths and decorations. The *1936 Household Searchlight Homemaking Guide* advised that "Buffet services and bridge games should have colorful gaily printed linens." It also noted that "The family dinner is laid with a gay cloth in as bright a design as desired, the family meal should be an informal and happy occasion." This was a big change from the earlier strict etiquette of the 1920s, which had dictated the use of the plain white damask or lace tablecloth for the family dinner table.

The Sears Catalogue from 1936 showed a large variety of printed tablecloths, many still the traditional white and colored damasks and linen plaids in blue, orange, green, and brown. But it also showed many new colorful printed patterns, which were available for the family dinner table. The sizes of printed tablecloths also began to change, with the "breakfast cloth" 28" or 30" square, the "luncheon cloth" 32" or 45" square, and the "dinner or supper cloth" 54" or 70" square.

Despite the extreme hardship of the Depression, Americans forged ahead during the '30s. They were infatuated with motion, speed, and travel. If Americans couldn't find work, at least they could go for a drive, have a cigarette, or go to a movie. Correspondingly, sales of oil, gas, cigarettes, and movie tickets all went up. Americans took to the road by car with the opening of Route 66, which enabled people to travel across the United States from Chicago to Los Angeles. Souvenir tablecloths became increasingly popular as collectibles.

> We're the first nation in the history of the world to go to the poorhouse in an automobile.
> —Humorist Will Rogers

Mosse Linen advertisement.

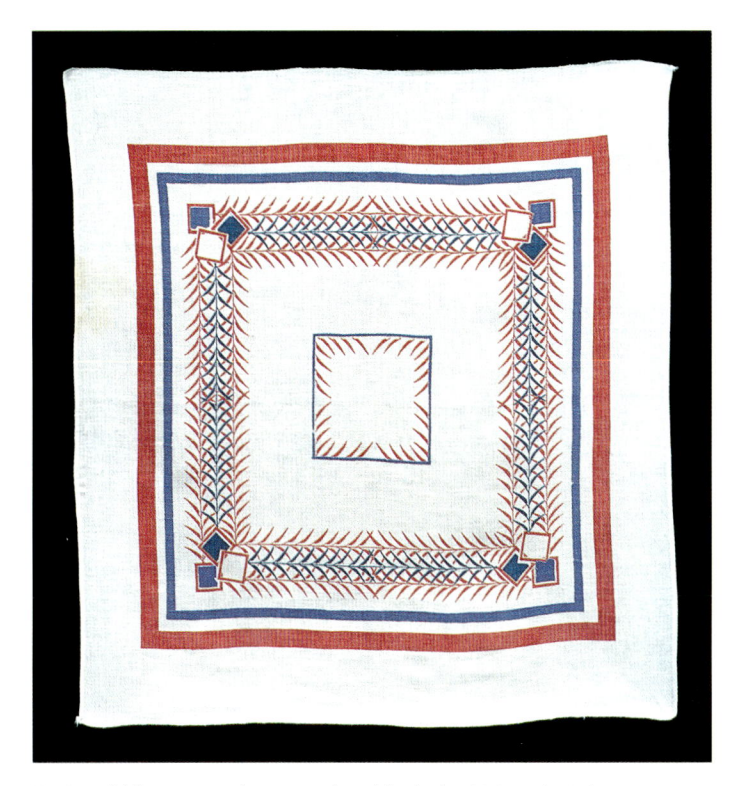

Red and blue unusual geometric tablecloth, 1930s. $40-$55.

Red and blue large printed stylized floral on linen, early 1930s. $50-$75.

Soft pink grapes and ribbons flow across this late 1930s tablecloth. $45-$55.

Blue flowers, brown leaves, and flowing ribbons on a textured heavy cotton tablecloth, classic 1930s themes. $50-$75.

The Depression: 1930s   31

Darling red clover and checks feedsack tablecloth and napkins. This pattern is similar to a Simtex "red clover" pattern, circa 1930s. $50-$75.

Soft blue strawberry tablecloth, my grandmother's favorite, late 1930s. $50-$75.

Early two color fruit linen tablecloth; unused, it still retains its vivid colors. Example of tablecloth showing colors that are opposites on the color wheel, 1930s. $75-$125.

Soft pink and blue florals grace each corner of this delightful tablecloth, late 1930s. $50-$75.

Unusual urn and floral themed tablecloth, wonderful "depression green" color, late 1930s. $55-95.

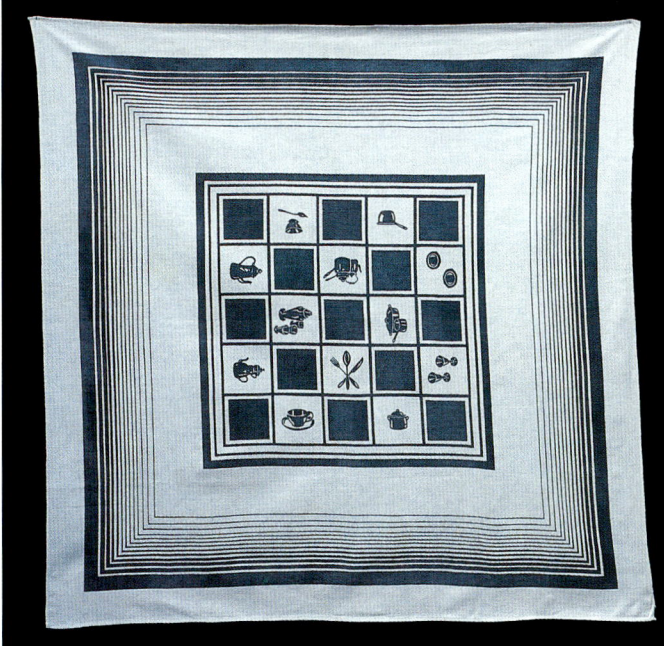

Depression era green kitchen tablecloth. Deep dark green color was a favorite for the late 1930s. $50-$75.

Fabulous faded blue and red fruit print, early 1930s. $45-$55.

The Depression: 1930s   33

Rare Springmaid "Spring Maid" boxed tablecloth, given only to Springmaid employees as a Christmas present by Elliott Springs, President, circa 1937-1941. $500-$750.

Rare Springmaid "Spring Maid" boxed napkin set, given only to Springmaid employees as a Christmas present by Elliott Springs, President, circa 1937-1941. $275-$350.

Rare Springmaid "Spring Maid" tablecloth, circa 1937-1941 (without box, $175-$225).

34 The Depression: 1930s

Pink and blue surreal angels, horsemen, and trees, 1930s. $50-$75.

Bright fiesta colors in a delightful Mexican themed, late 1930s tablecloth. $50-$75.

Oriental themed bamboo tablecloth in pinks and grays, circa 1930s. $45-$50.

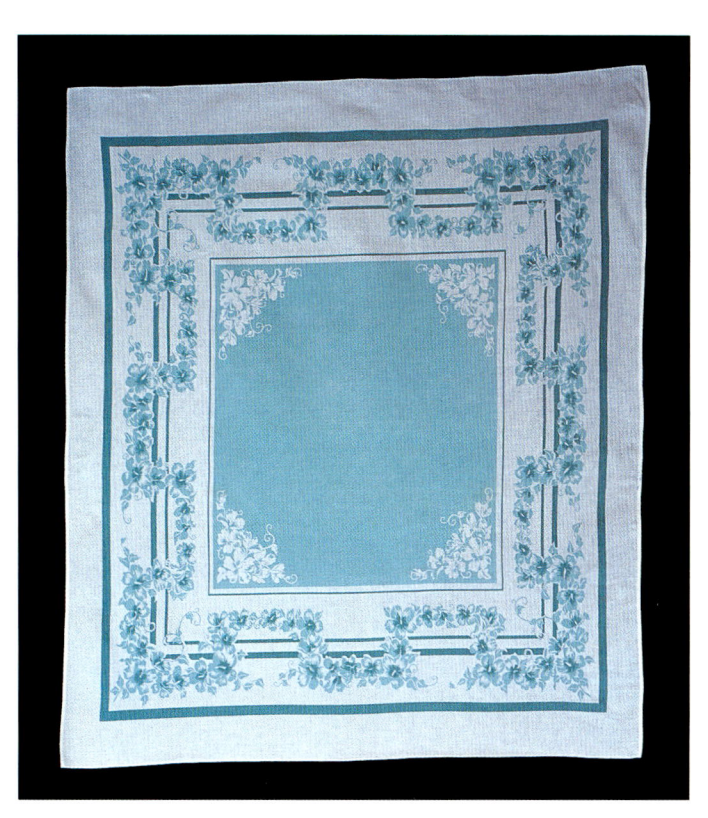

A cool blue-green floral, an elegant tablecloth, late 1930s. $45-$75.

The Depression: 1930s 35

One color, Utah state souvenir tablecloth, 1930s. Dated using national parks and other landmarks, circa 1928-1935. $100-$125.

Sweet ribbons and flowers in a resist dyed pattern, late 1930s. $30-$55.

Mint condition California state tablecloth, produced by R.A McFarland in the late 1930s. Photographed on the California coastline. $150-$195.

Another view of the California state tablecloth.

36   The Depression: 1930s

Marion Van Dorn designer tablecloth, subtle colors in a dramatic oriental theme, late 1930s. $50-$75.

Signature of designer Marion V. Dorn.

Margaret Newport designed California state tablecloth, late 1930s. $55-$75.

Signature of designer Margaret Newport.

The Depression: 1930s 37

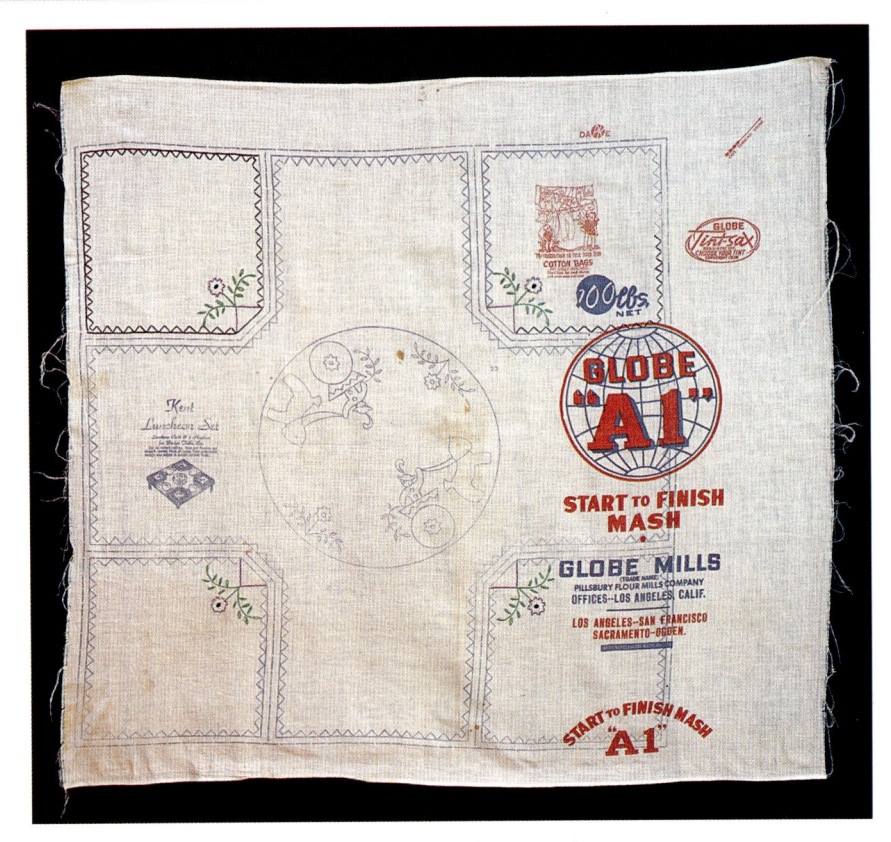

Feedsack 1936 "Globe A-1 Tint-sax" tablecloth pattern for "Kent Luncheon set." Unwashed, it still shows the pattern, manufacturer, and directions. Fabulous graphics. $125-$175.

Globe Tint-sax label.

Directions for embroidering the "Kent Luncheon set."

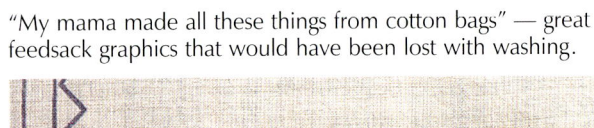

"My mama made all these things from cotton bags" — great feedsack graphics that would have been lost with washing.

38   The Depression: 1930s

Yellow roses and red leaves with a flowing ribbon border, early 1930s. $75-$95.

Dramatic teal green and brown floral tablecloth, late 1930s. $55-$75.

Red, brown, and lime green accents in a stunning oriental theme, late 1930s. $100-$125.

Soft and subtle flowers edge this gray and yellow 1930s tablecloth. $75-$100.

The Depression: 1930s 39

Gold cattails and water lilies frame this delightful tablecloth from the 1930s. $50-$65.

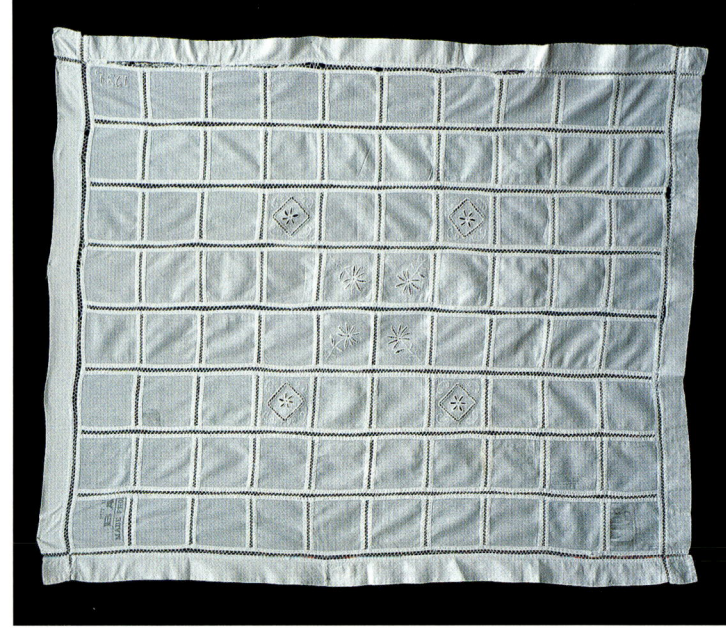

Feedsack tablecloth, dated 1934. Pieced from small squares of bleached feedsack and crocheted together. Evidence of original manufacturer's lettering makes this a wonderful piece of kitchen history. $150-$175.

Early 1930s deep red printed oriental themed tablecloth. $75-$100.

Romantic magnolias and colors opposite the color wheel date this to the 1930s. Note the large print with large wide edges. $75-$100.

40   The Depression: 1930s

Terra cotta daffodils and apple blossoms make an enchanting late 1930s tablecloth. $50-$75.

Wonderful fall theme of scattered leaves in maroon, late 1930s. $50-$75.

Concentric stripes and floral design in blue and red on a crisp linen, 1930s. $45-$55.

Sweet blue tulips, sage green leaves, and a dark red border make a darling small breakfast cloth, late 1930s. $50-$75.

The Depression: 1930s 41

Linen pink and blue florals makes a soft and inviting tablecloth, late 1930s. $50-$75.

Dark blue and maroon floral and fern tablecloth, late 1930s. $50-$75.

Romantic flowing pink and blue floral tablecloth on heavy sailcloth, late 1930s. $75-$100.

A small red and blue floral and plaid tablecloth, 1930s. Note the darker red, which is indicative of an early red dye. $50-$75.

Victory K&B Apple Blossom tablecloth; they call it "Leaf." Note the brown and blue leaves, larger print characteristic of early 1930s tablecloths. $75-$125.

Close-up of Victory K&B tablecloth with tag.

Dark red and blue flowers with yellow stems, an early 1930s beauty. $55-$75.

A strawberry patterned tablecloth, soft reds and purples make this a sweet cloth, late 1930s. $50-$75.

The Depression: 1930s 43

Deco inspired blue, gold, and browns create a flowing, elegant design, 1930s. $50-$75.

Mint Deerfield Quality Product manufactured floral tablecloth. Overprinted design of pink, green, and maroon, late 1930s. $75-$100.

Cool sage green acorn and leaf tablecloth, 1930s. $55-$65.

Stunning deco maroon and blue floral garlands makes an elegant tablecloth, 1930s. $100-$125.

Mint condition, green and orange "Art Deco" tablecloth, a rare find, 1930s. Unused, it still retains its original colors. $100-$150.

44   The Depression: 1930s

Wonderful Mexican themed tablecloth. Green, one color, screen printed, late 1930s. *From the collection of Marith Willis.* $75-$100.

Heavy block printed floral tablecloth on sailcloth. Uneven color distribution in the pattern will help determine this printing process, 1930. $55-$75.

Fabulous "Prohibition era" Black Americana luncheon tablecloth, early 1930s. $200-$250.

Close-up of the fun Prohibition design.

The Depression: 1930s 45

Chapter 7
World War II: 1940s

Large fruits in 12" repeating squares, a wonderful picnic tablecloth, early 1940s. $65-$80.

Although America was not yet in the war when the decade began, many textile and dye resources were already being directed towards the nation's eventual allies. This shortage had a tremendous impact on tablecloth production. Percales, white broadcloth, batiste, and cotton all "went to war" and the fabrics that were available were of poor quality and not colorfast. The government forced American textile manufacturers to substitute other fibers for domestic uses, resulting in an increased use of nylon blends. The government influenced tablecloth manufacturers in other ways as well. For example, I found an interesting vintage strawberry tablecloth with four matching napkins still in its original box, with an "OPA" price sticker. This was the mark of the "Office of Price Administration," a government price control agency that functioned to keep prices from skyrocketing during World War II. This agency created a general maximum-price regulation, which determined prices that were charged in March 1942 as the ceiling prices for most commodities. Because of this mark, we know this sweet strawberry tablecloth can be dated between 1941 and 1947.

The hard times of the Depression faded as many workers found jobs in war-oriented factories and people found a renewed self-assuredness and patriotism about all things American. Labels from the early 1940s to the 1950s proudly stated "Made in the USA" or "Made in America." With a significant proportion of mill production diverted to war use, the "hand printed" tablecloth produced by small tablecloth manufacturers was in vogue and provided new opportunities for several California companies like California Hand Prints, Yucca Prints, and Calaprints to compete in what was once a larger market.

New techniques and advancements in the printing process also created "new roller printed cloths." The 1940-41 Sears Catalogue advertised: "Never before has a complete pattern been roller printed on this size cloth! Makes the colors fast to both sun and tub. Brings out the intricate shadings and clear-cut designs. Improvements never dreamed of under the old process." Prior to 1940, tablecloths had featured larger corner prints, or smaller prints around the edges of the cloth, usually on a 54" x 54" or smaller cloth. After this date, tablecloths were produced with more complex designs, subtle shadings, and an increased numbers of colors used for the designs. However, early 1940s tablecloths still showed a more one dimensional or flat design. It was not until around 1948 that the tablecloths showed the more three dimensional look, with multi-faceted colors and more complex shading in the leaf and flower prints.

American ingenuity and thrift were practiced with food and all items used in the home and then everything changed. The war was won and the economy and the population was booming. Americans were healthier, happier, better educated, and far more affluent than ever before. Millions of homes were built for returning GIs and their new brides. Many women, who had worked for the first time during the war, continued to work, adding extra income to the family. Many households bought their first stoves, refrigerators, washing machines, and bigger cars.

George Numann and his wife Vera were very successful in 1936 in California with their small hand printed textile firms, Printex and Vera. "Vera" tablecloths were popular from the mid 1940s to late 1970s and always featured her signature mark in the corner of the design.

The mid to late 1940s were the "heyday" of the cotton printed tablecloth. The majority of tablecloths found today were produced during this time. The sheer diversity of colors and the styles that were produced are amazing. Most popular tablecloth designs were offered in many color variations and fabrics like linen, cotton, or rayon. They were produced to coordinate with the family's china patterns and kitchen décor. Since women had entered the workforce during the war, they had less time to make their own tablecloths from yard goods fabrics. More tablecloths began to be produced by a variety of new manufacturers, responding to this market demand. Simtex, Hardy Craft, Belcrest Prints, Rosemary Products, as well as scores of others all created colorfully printed tablecloths during this period. Rosemary Products often marked their early tablecloths with their signature "flower" trademark. It is almost incorporated into the design and is often difficult to see unless you look closely.

The Springs Cotton Mills, a well known textile manufacturer, expanded their textile operations with great success and opened a "finishing house" in 1946 to create and market their line of printed tablecloths. Most of their patterns were florals printed on lightweight Egyptian cotton fabrics — crisp, bright and very popular. Eager to capitalize on the popularity of the printed tablecloth, Sears created its own line of tablecloths under the name "Harmony House" and J.C. Penney started their "Pennicraft" label. Both were profitable labels and were featured prominently in their catalogs. Most of the collectible tablecloths you can find today were made during this prosperous time.

Voluntarily adhering to a label standard, some tablecloth manufacturers began sewing tags into their products to identify the makers. Startex also began promoting their lines of elegant, rich damasks and wonderful gaily printed tablecloths in colorful full-page advertisements. Their desire was to encourage market loyalty to their product. They sewed a tag on their tablecloths and produced print media advertisements showing wonderful printed tablecloths being used with the typical happy American family gathered at the table. The ads included sayings such as, "Thrifty for your family, charming for your friends," and "Simtex cloths are bright and right for either morning or night!" Consumers were asked to "look for the garnet and gray Simtex Made Right in America label." Consumers responded with delight. Soon Simtex was one of the most popular lines of tablecloths and today it is still a favorite of vintage tablecloth collectors for its bold designs and durable fabrics.

Simtex advertisement for damask tablecloths. *With permission from WestPoint Stevens Inc.*

Simtex advertisement for plaid and checked tablecloths. *With permission from WestPoint Stevens Inc.*

Left:
Simtex Easter advertisement. *With permission from WestPoint Stevens Inc.*

Right:
Simtex Christmas advertisement. *With permission from WestPoint Stevens Inc.*

48 World War II: 1940s

Simtex advertisement showing "Strawberry Patch" tablecloth. *With permission from WestPoint Stevens Inc.*

Simtex advertisement showing "Pueblo" tablecloth. *With permission from WestPoint Stevens Inc.*

Simtex advertisement showing fruit pattern tablecloth. *With permission from WestPoint Stevens Inc.*

World War II: 1940s 49

The most popular size of luncheon tablecloths during this time was 54" square. Bridge or tea tablecloths were 34" x 36". The consumer demand for easy care tablecloths led to tablecloth manufacturers using terms like "Sanforized" or "Sandforset" to denote shrinkage control, and "Mercanization" for durability. According to Isabel Wingate in her 1949 book *Textile Fabrics and Their Selection*, the chief selling points for tablecloths during this time were "appearance, suitability, serviceability, durability, launderability, and size." After collecting and actually using these vintage tablecloths, I can understand her advice. The early linen and Egyptian cotton tablecloths are incredibly hard to keep wrinkle and stain free. I much prefer the rayon-cotton blends, which retain their shape and color and are easy to launder.

Woodsy themes incorporating pinecones, aspens, and forest designs were in vogue briefly after the war. Stylized fragrant florals and dogwood blossoms were favorites, as well as calendulas, hibiscus, orchids, lily of the valley, and other lush tropical prints. Also found were plaids with a wide band of color and picnic checks. Cartoon prints were popular, along with tablecloths rich in figural imaginative regional images featuring cute children and Carmen Miranda type prints. Western, farm inspired, and Black Americana designs flooded the market.

Mexican themes were also popular, to coordinate with the fashionable Homer Laughlin "Fiesta" china patterns that were produced in the late 1930s. The 1947 Sears catalogue featured several Fiesta coordinating household yard goods prints: "A smart 'Fiesta' print yardage that lends itself so well to complete decorative schemes because of its extra width. Buy enough for a tablecloth, window curtain, towels, aprons and chair pad sets and see how your kitchen sparkles with color." These tablecloths are still prized today by Fiesta collectors for their vivid colors and Mexican themes and are widely available to collectors.

The Wilendur "Strawberry" pattern was also featured in the 1947 Sears catalogue, with the following description: "Luscious, ripe red strawberries and cool green leaves on a background of crisp white. What could be more inviting in a kitchen or dinette than this? The strawberry print cotton yardage is a big favorite because it's extra heavy. It's gay, colorful and so practical you can make dozens of things." This popular pattern was offered in three widths: 17" toweling, 36" toweling, and 54" tablecloth. Both Wilendur and Simtex also marketed a set of coordinating "Matkins" that could be napkins or placemats, depending on how you wanted to use them. In addition, they created tablecloth and napkin boxed sets, some with a pink or red stitched border and some packaged with coordinating painted metal lunch trays. Most Wilendur patterned tablecloths are still available in large quantities due to their immense popularity. As well as looking fabulous on a table, they are also prized for their bold, bright patterns, arranged in 14" or 16" squares, and heavy cotton materials that make wonderful hand crafted tablecloth pillows and other craft items.

Lush and plentiful fruit and vegetable as well as farm themed prints were very popular for their symbolism of the harvest and riches of the earth. During World War II, every home had a "Victory Garden" and these fabulous tablecloths are great examples of the bountiful mood that characterized most post war Americans. It is interesting to note that this is also the time when rural country and farm life was rapidly diminishing in favor of encroaching, affordable tract housing developments and expanding city limits. In 1900, 80% of Americans lived in rural areas. By the late 1940s, 80% were living in large cities.

Tablecloth manufacturers began to produce coordinated kitchen lines of items for the kitchen. There were utensils, containers, tablecloths, tea towels, curtains, and even stick-on decals for the cabinets. Tablecloths were produced and boxed in "Luncheon and Tea Sets" for the smaller tables, and in larger sizes for the family dinner table. It was now fashionable to use these brightly printed tablecloths for elaborate dinner parties and other social gatherings. The boxed sets were given as gifts for birthdays and weddings and can occasionally still be found in their original packaging, sometimes with the gift card attached. When these are discovered it is a rare and special treat for the tablecloth collector.

Although state souvenir tablecloths were produced as early as the 1930s, they rapidly increased in popularity in the late 1940s as more people traveled by car and train to see the United States. By the late 1940s, the combination of consumer demand and new production reinvigorated the American car culture. The price of gasoline fell and the family car became more affordable. The war, as well as the increased number of motorists, facilitated the construction of a cross continental roadway system. Americans were eager to take to the road to discover America, buying souvenirs from the states they visited along the way.

All states at one time sold souvenir tablecloths and tea towels. You could also find a tablecloth featuring the "western states" and one picturing the entire United States on one cloth. The earlier state tablecloths were smaller, usually 34" or 38", and not as detailed as the later ones. By the late 1940s, state tablecloths were being produced in larger sizes of 52" and 64", with coordinating napkins for use at the family kitchen table.

The most highly sought after state tablecloths are those from the mid west states, such as North and South Dakota, Kansas, and Ohio. Since these states and others were not as popular as other tourist destinations, the tablecloths are harder to find and can be valued as high as $375. California, Florida, New York, Alaska, Nevada, Hawaii, and Wyoming, as well as the states that Route 66 cut through, were the most popular destinations. These souvenir state tablecloths are easier for the collector to acquire. Occasionally, you will find a Startex or Simtex label on these tablecloths, demonstrating their immense popularity, as the large tablecloth manufacturers responded to the market demand. It is easy to find these tablecloths with their original tags and in unused condition, since they were put away after the family returned from vacation. Yucca Prints and Cactus Cloth were usually sold at newsstands and these manufacturers seem to be the most popular producers of these vintage pieces of state history.

Souvenir tablecloths were also produced to showcase popular tourist destinations. You can find tablecloths featuring "Lake Michigan" and "Yellowstone Park" as well as "Washington D.C." and "Los Angeles," just to name a few. They were produced to show the local attractions and highlights. These are a little harder to come by and are a delightful addition to state souvenir tablecloth collections.

It is easy to date souvenir tablecloths by researching the tourist attractions shown; sometimes the general date can be determined by which landmarks are pictured on the cloth. In California, for example, "Boulder Dam" changed its name to "Hoover Dam" in 1947 and Disneyland opened in 1955. With regard to Florida tablecloths, Walt Disney World didn't open until 1971. The Utah State tablecloth shown in the previous chapter can be dated to the early 1930s by looking at the national parks: Dinosaur National Monument was established in 1932, and Zion and Bryce national parks (misspelled on this tablecloth as "brice") were established prior to that. This tablecloth also highlights some attractions that were only popular in the late 1920s and early 1930s. For example, "Bingham Canyon" was a mining town in the 1920s. Auto racing in the Great Salt Lake basin was popular from 1914 to the 1930s. Peach produce farms were a thriving industry in Utah until the late 1930s. This is a great example of an early one-color 1930s state souvenir tablecloth.

State souvenir tablecloths are examples of a "cross collectible." Both the vintage printed tablecloth collector and the souvenir collector share a love for these pieces of American memorabilia. Several other types of tablecloths are also of interest as "cross collectibles." Black Americana, western, signed "designer prints," and cartoon print themes are extremely sought after by a wide variety of collectors, and the prices rise correspondingly with the ever-increasing demand from a cross section of collectors.

Simtex "Strawberry Patch" tablecloth, as featured in their 1948 ad (see page 49). $75-$100.

Classic 1940s fruit pattern in repeating grid and primary colors, gorgeous, 1940s. $55-$75.

Soft green and red fruits combined with romantic florals make a wonderful tablecloth, early 1940s. $50-$75.

World War II: 1940s 51

Delicious strawberries surround a reverse printed floral center stripe, late 1940s. $80-$120.

My grandmother's bountiful fruit tablecloth, childhood memories make this priceless to me, early 1940s. $50-$75.

Juicy blue grapes trail off this heavy cotton tablecloth, early 1940s. $75-$100.

Stamped repeating fruit design on heavy cotton, early 1940s. $50-$75.

52   World War II: 1940s

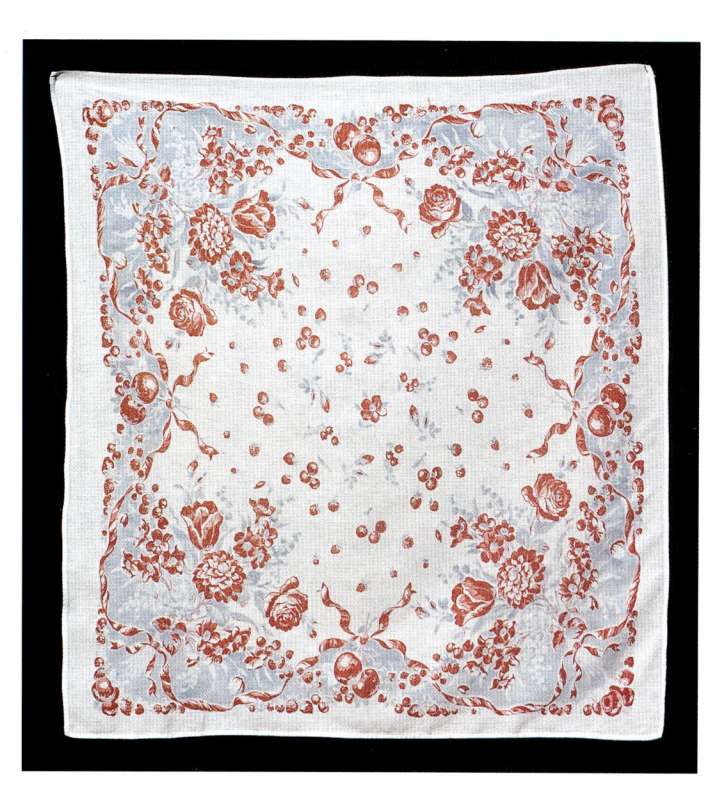

Delicious blue and soft green fruits in small repeating patterns, very "shabby chic," 1940s. $75-$95.

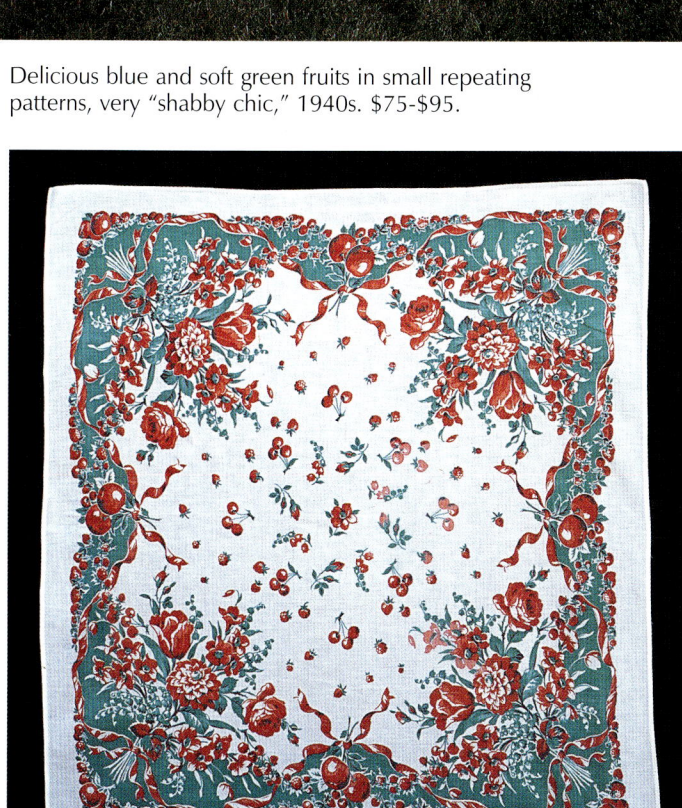

Soft faded blue and red fruit and florals. A darling breakfast tablecloth, early 1940s. $50-$75.

Green and red floral bouquets, apples, and cherries theme. It also came in blue and usually is very faded due to unstable dyes, early 1940s. $50-$75.

Gorgeous grapes and leaves highlight this early 1940s tablecloth. $75-$90.

World War II: 1940s 53

"Roof tops and fruits" classic 1940s themes of home, church, and bountiful fruits make this an interesting, unusual tablecloth. $75-$125.

Parisian Prints vivid vegetable tablecloth. Influenced by Word War II "victory gardens," this tablecloth reflects the bountiful mood of post war America, late 1940s. $150-$175.

Mint Callaway produced wonderful grape tablecloth, an example of their excellence in tablecloth design, late 1940s. $100-$125.

Close-up of Callaway signature.

54 World War II: 1940s

Darling vegetable tablecloth, most likely a "second." You can see where the bolts of gray goods fabrics were sewn together to make continuous printing possible. $45-$55.

Close-up of seam in the vegetable tablecloth.

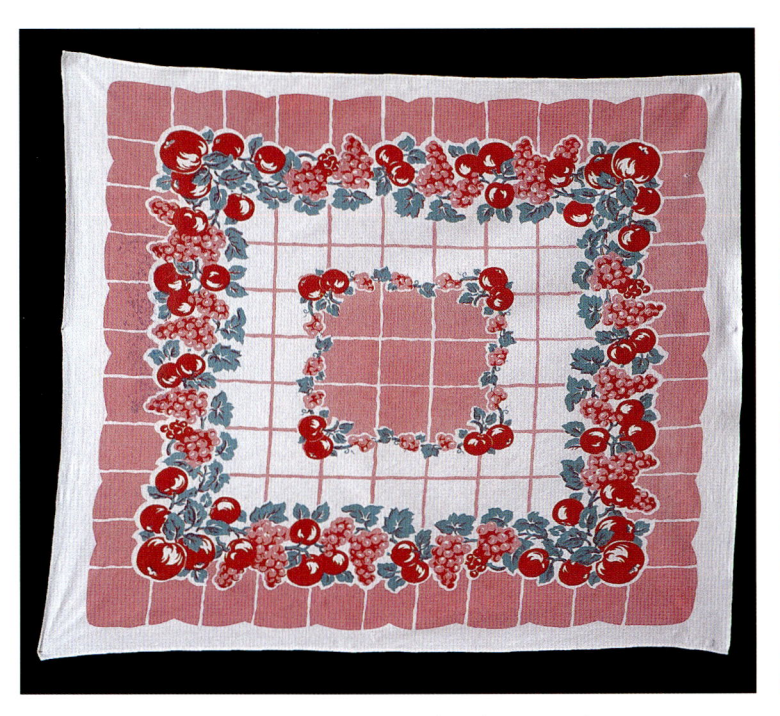

Darling pink fruit tablecloth. What makes this unusual is the "Dixiana Motel" mark. Possibly a "taken" souvenir from a vacation, early 1940s. $95-$100.

Property mark of the "Dixiana Motel."

World War II: 1940s   55

Deep red cherries and green leaves cover this darling tablecloth, 1940s. $80-$125.

Sweet strawberries are scattered across this classic late 1940s tablecloth. $75-$95.

Fresh Wilendur fiesta fruits in primary colors with yellow border, early 1940s. $70-$80.

Fiesta themed fruit baskets, bold colors on textured cotton, late 1940s. $60-$75.

This stunning tablecloth has all the popular 1940s themes — fruits, tropical florals, and little scenes of boats and beaches nestled into the design. $75-$100.

Close-up of the tiny scenes.

Beautiful blue tulips in alternating reverse printed and colored design highlight a delightful checked center, 1940s. $75-$95.

1940s blue and white leaf and acorn repeating pattern. $60-$75.

World War II: 1940s 57

California Hand Prints "Peony" cool oriental influenced floral design. Stunning, rich colors, late 1940s. $75-$85.

Linen dogwood floral tablecloth in blue, also came in pink, yellow, and brown color choices, late 1940s. $55-$75.

Pale blue stripes with pink roses create a wonderful summer tablecloth, late 1940s. $45-$75.

Yellow flowers in a well ordered grid pattern, late 1940s $55-$75.

Brown and yellow sunny poppy print. Came in red, blue, brown, orange colors, late 1940s. $75-$95.

Weil & Durrse's red rose tablecloth with their America's Pride label, same pattern as their Wilendur label, late 1940s. $95-$150.

Wilendur apple blossom patterned tablecloth, late 1940s. $75-$125.

Lancaster Prints. A red floral beauty, 1940s. $50-$75.

World War II: 1940s 59

Lavender pansies, geometric shapes, and patterns. A visually interesting tablecloth, late 1940s. $50-$75.

Brilliant bold florals bring a summer garden to the table, 1940s. $75-$100.

Unusual pine branches set against a lime green background, wonderful western feel, late 1940s. $75-$100.

Sweet gold poppies, soft butterflies, and other spring flowers grace this lovely colored linen tablecloth, late 1940s. $50-$75.

Mint Wilendur soft pink roses in their classic "Royal Rose" luncheon set with napkins, 1940s. $125-$150.

Wilendur "Royal Rose" tag.

Graceful red and yellow gladiolas frame a blue/green background, early 1940s. $50-$65.

Wilendur "Poppy" tablecloth. Vivid poppies and heavy cotton. A collector favorite for crafting and display, early 1940s. $50-$75.

World War II: 1940s 61

Tropical floral overprinted tablecloth. First the pale blue was printed, then the red floral to make purple, early 1940s. $75-$100.

Bold red and blue florals and a crisp geometric design. Made by Wifitex in the late 1940s. $75-$100.

Elegant roses trail around the edges of this late cool green 1940s beauty. $45-$65.

Mint Queen Anne, Indian Head manufactured, stunning blue roses make an elegant tablecloth, late 1940s. $100-$125.

62 World War II: 1940s

Exciting primary color floral and stripes tablecloth, 1940s. $75-$100.

Lime green and pink cherry blossoms, an oriental influenced design of subtle beauty, early 1940s. $60-$75.

Delicious fruits and pale pinks make this a soft and inviting tablecloth, late 1940s. $75-$100.

Exotic florals and leaves cover this visually interesting heavy linen tablecloth, early 1940s. $75-$100.

World War II: 1940s　63

Simtex's colorful, luscious tropical hibiscus tablecloth, late 1940s. $75-$100.

Darling bright florals with uneven fading to the blue edge, most likely bleach damage, early 1940s. $50-$75.

Rows of individual spring flowers combine in the center to make a beautiful bouquet, late 1940s. $75-$100.

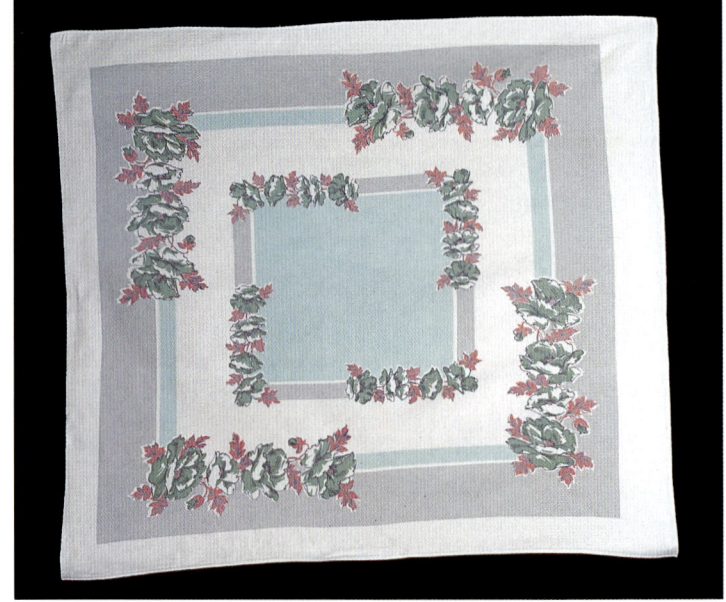

Subdued gray, green, and pink florals, interesting use of green for roses and pink for the leaves, early 1940s. $50-$75.

Teal, gold, and blue teapots, sailboats, and floral themes, "the good life" late 1940s linen tablecloth. $50-$75.

Charming red and yellow spring flowers, a real treasure for your kitchen, 1940s. $75-$100.

Springmaid, a Lancaster Print tablecloth of stunning blue roses with red accents. You will find this most often in faded condition, 1940s. $50-$75.

Delightful primary colored tropical theme, a 1940s classic. $75-$100.

World War II: 1940s 65

Wonderful tulips and other spring flowers burst with color on this crisp Egyptian cotton tablecloth from the 1940s. $45-$55.

Bold tulips with a Greek key edge makes a gorgeous tablecloth from the early 1940s. *From the collection of Marith Willis.* $75-$100.

ML Cloths "Flower Basket," beautiful two color early 1940s design. $75-$100.

Soft blue morning glories and lavender ribbons play across this delightful tablecloth, early 1940s. $75-$100.

66   World War II: 1940s

Muted maroon and blue floral pattern on a light Egyptian cotton tablecloth, early 1940s. $45-$50.

Wilendur "American Beauty" pattern tablecloth, came in boxed sets and home yard goods cloth, late 1940s. $75-$100.

Block printed, fruit patterned breakfast cloth, uneven colors and patterns give us the clue as to the printing process, early 1940s. $45-$55.

Sunny tulips and other florals accented with delightful checks, early 1940s. $75-$100.

World War II: 1940s 67

Red and blue tablecloth in a chintz, tropical floral theme, early 1940s. $55-$75.

Stunning pink and maroon florals set against a gray background, late 1940s. $75-$100.

Sweet pink roses set against a gray lacey ribbon, very "shabby chic," 1940s. $50-$75.

Springmaid classic floral made in their Lancaster plant, also came in blue, 1940s. $50-$75.

California Hand Prints "pinecone" tablecloth, wonderful color combinations and theme, early 1940s. $65-$75.

There is nothing more wonderful than a red and white polka dot tablecloth, great for layering, early 1940s. $75-$100.

Delicate pink cherry blossoms in an oriental influenced design, late 1940s $50-$75.

Linen "apple blossom" tablecloth in blues, also came in yellow and pink, early 1940s. $50-$75.

World War II: 1940s 69

Stalwart brand (a Macy's brand) tag.

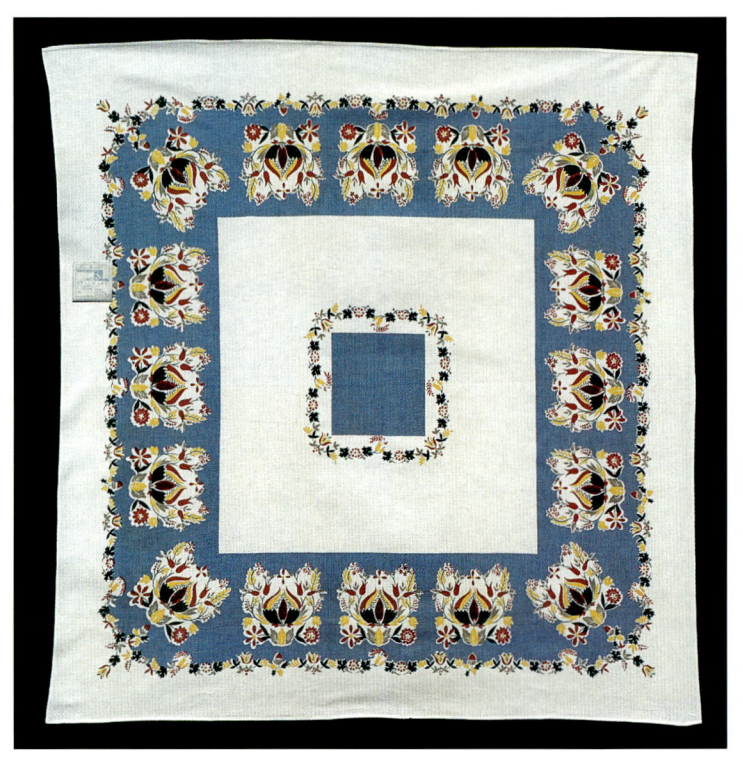

Mint Stalwart brand Pennsylvania Dutch inspired stylized floral. Offered at Macy's in the 1940s. $75-$95.

Startex "red clover" patterned tablecloth. Cute for Valentine's Day, early 1940s. $50-$65.

Different shades of mauve highlight this darling daisy tablecloth, early 1940s. $50-$75.

Delicate white floral swags decorate the edge of this 1940s tablecloth. $60-$75.

Romantic floral arrangements of bluebells and hydrangeas. A stunning tablecloth, late 1940s. $65-$95.

Scattered stylized floral patterned tablecloth, late 1940s. $50-$75.

Deep green leaves of all types decorate this lush tablecloth, late 1940s. $50-$75.

World War II: 1940s 71

Springmaid, "St Regis" blue geranium tablecloth, 1940s. $60-$75.

Springmaid "St Regis" tag.

Mint Springmaid "St Regis" red geranium tablecloth, 1940s. $60-$75.

Hardy Craft. Clusters of spring flowers grace this darling linen tablecloth, late 1940s. $55-$75.

Red and blue roses make a romantic tablecloth, late 1940s. $50-$75.

White cherry blossom branches scattered across a pink linen tablecloth, late 1940s. $45-$65.

A romantic floral tablecloth that takes your breath away with its gentle beauty, early 1940s. $100-$125.

Close-up of the stunning floral pattern.

World War II: 1940s

Beautiful bright black-eyed Susan tablecloth. A Radiant Beauty manufactured tablecloth, late 1940s. $65-$95.

California Hand Prints muted browns, green and pinks give this tablecloth a quiet elegance. Narco rayon blend, late 1940s. $65-$75.

Radiant Beauty Table Cloth tag.

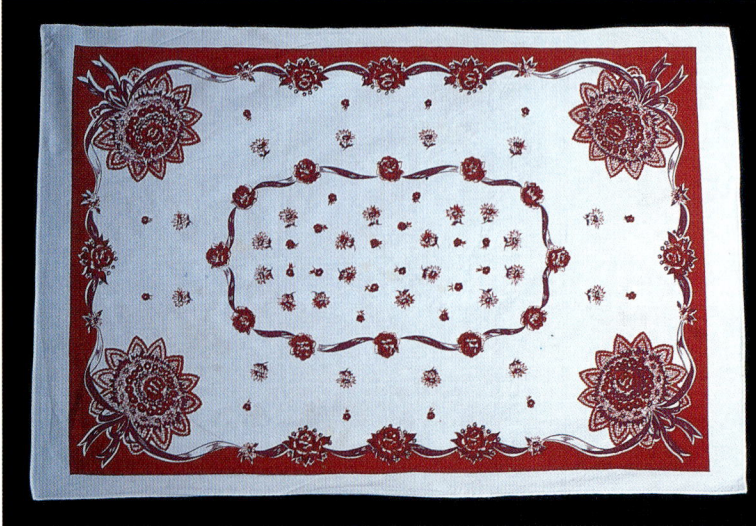

Deep red lacy heart doilies and flowers make this a perfect Valentine's tablecloth, late 1940s. $55-$75.

74   World War II: 1940s

Sunny yellow floral tablecloth, pictured with the Bolivar, Missouri, Volunteer Fire Department vintage fire trucks, late 1940s. $50-$75.

Glorious Startex poppy and daisy tablecloth, late 1940s. $95-$125.

Faded pink stripes overprinted with rose floral clusters, late 1940s. $45-$75.

Mint Tokyo imported floral linen tablecloth, early 1940s, most likely not used due to the war. $50-$75.

World War II: 1940s 75

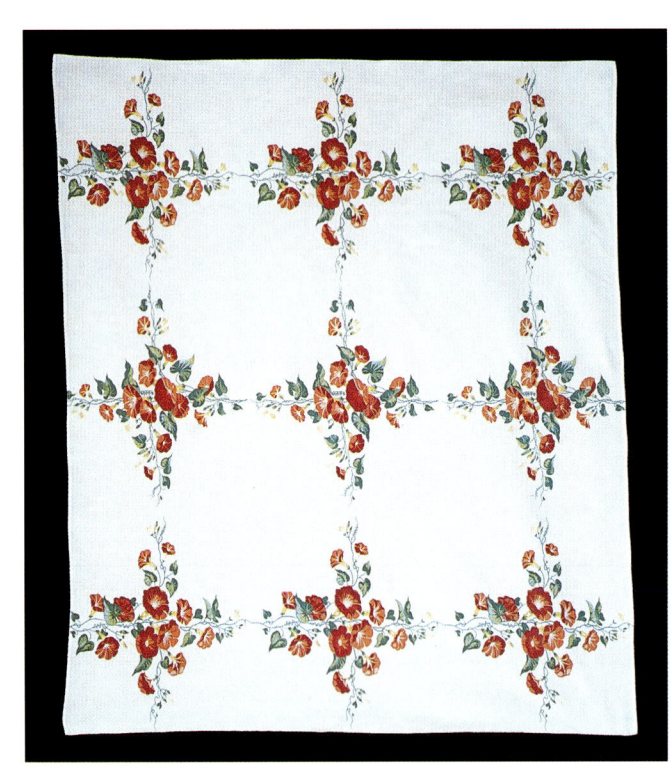

Wilendur "Morning Glory" tablecloth. Faded background of yellow plaid is evident, late 1940s. $40-$70.

Pale blue and mauve floral tablecloth. Came in yellow, red, and blue colors, early 1940s. $55-$75.

Dark blues, pink, and an "early" green make this a wonderful, simple floral tablecloth, early 1940s. $55-$75.

Sweet muted colors of spring flowers and ribbons highlight this tablecloth, late 1940s. $50-$75.

Mint Gribbon "Cosmos" linen tablecloth in brown, late 1940s. $60-$75.

Corner spring bouquets and romantic flowing ribbons, early 1940s. $65-$75.

Victory K&B "Clokay no iron" tablecloth. This design was featured in the 1946 Sears catalog. It is an unusual cotton vinyl coated tablecloth, for easy care. $40-$50.

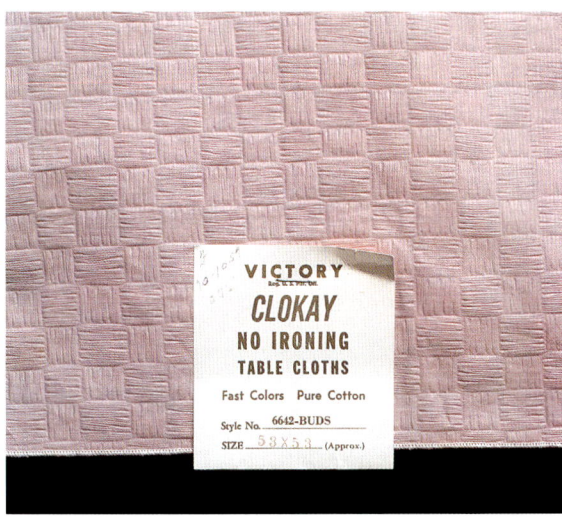

Victory K&B "Clokay" tag.

World War II: 1940s   77

Mint Rosemary Stylecraft Prints tablecloth in their "Gaiety" pattern, early 1940s. $50-$75.

Rosemary Stylecraft Prints tag.

Decorative Linens (OLC) tag.

Decorative Linens (OLC) overprinted red and blue to try to create a purple color, early 1940s. $55-$75.

Romantic florals and ribbons make a quietly elegant tablecloth, early 1940s. $50-$75.

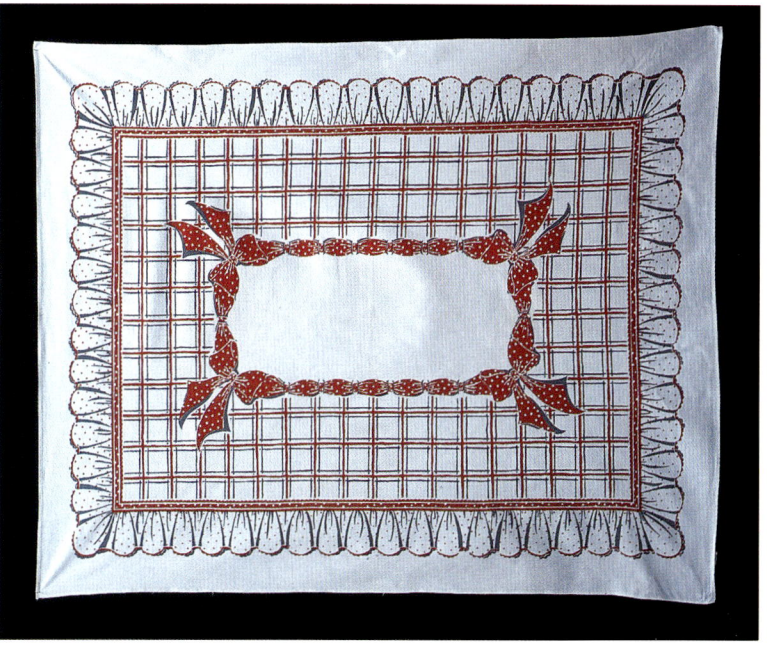

Darling polka dots, checks, and ribbons tablecloth. This was featured in the 1946 Sears catalog for $1.98. $55-$75.

Mint Simtex "Carnation" tablecloth in their "sprout" color. Fun color combinations, late 1940s. $60-$75.

Simtex, Rosecraft tag.

World War II: 1940s 79

Charm Prints classic primary colored floral in 16" repeating squares, 1940s. $75-$85.

Charm Prints tag.

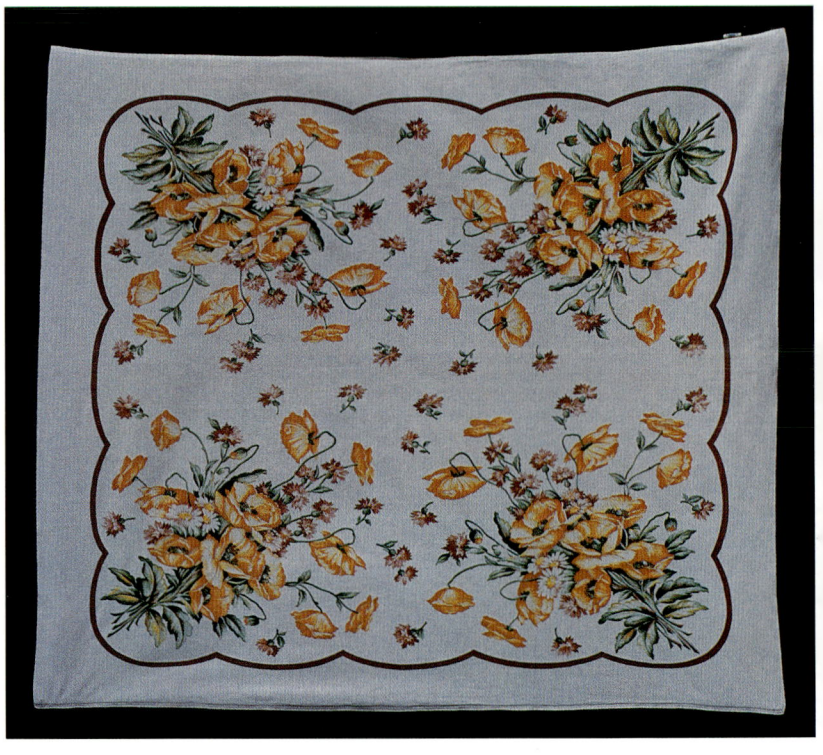

Sweet poppies in the corner make a wonderful spring tablecloth, late 1940s. $50-$75.

Exotic florals in a soft blue and red print, perfect for your garden tea party, early 1940s. $50-$75.

80 World War II: 1940s

Perfect pink and blue floral with delicate pussy willow edge. Heavy sailcloth, late 1940s. *From the collection of Marith Willis.* $100-$125.

Close-up of the perfect pink and blue floral with delicate pussy willow edge.

Soft Springmaid geranium tablecloth. This one is in almost mint condition, 1940s. $50-$75.

Stunning blue hydrangeas make an elegant statement for the dinner table, late 1940s. $75-$90.

World War II: 1940s   81

Red and blue tablecloth, with Victorian "gothic" influenced pattern, early 1940s. $60-$75.

Mint Stevens Hand Print brown and teal floral with delicate decorative edge design, late 1940s $60-$75.

Mint Springmaid "Lancaster Prints" scattered red spring flowers to brighten your table, late 1940s. $60-$75.

Springmaid "Lancaster Prints" spring floral tag.

Stevens Hand Print Table Cloth tag.

Classic Wilendur red dogwood breakfast tablecloth with matching table runner, 1940s. $75-$95.

Lime green Wilendur dogwood patterned tablecloth, late 1940s. $75-$95.

Wilendur "dogwood" tablecloth in four of the six colors, also came in black and yellow. The black is a rarer color, late 1940s. $75-$95.

World War II: 1940s 83

Cute Black Americana kitchen theme tablecloth, darling graphics, early 1940s. $150-$200.

Black Americana "plantation" tablecloth, lots of "Mammy" themes, this one is in poor condition, early 1940s. $75-$250.

Rosemary Products stylecraft prints tag.

Mint Rosemary "Tudor" patterned tablecloth, romantic cottage roses, late 1940s. $75-$95.

Unusual "saloon" tablecloth, risqué graphics. Belonged to a men's club card room, late 1940s. $75-$95.

Russian folk dancers playfully prance around this tablecloth, early 1940s. $75-$90.

"Wally" cartoon characters from the 1940s. An imaginative, whimsical rare picnic tablecloth. Heavy canvas, middle seam. $100-$125.

"Wally" signature.

World War II: 1940s 85

Stylized teapots and bricks in classic fiesta colors, late 1940s. $75-$95.

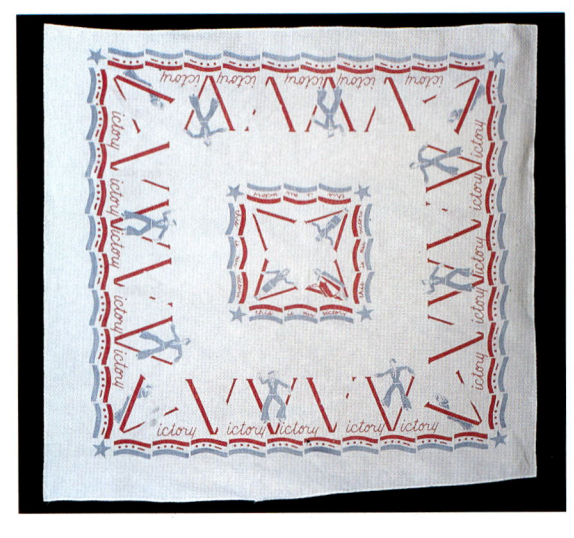

Jubilant "Victory" World War II tablecloth. Note the faded purple figures due to unstable war era dyes, 1946. $60-$75.

Close-up of farmer and wife tablecloth.

Farmer and his wife darling figural tablecloth. There is a definite "folk" influence in the design. This is an example of the post war bountiful mood of Americans, late 1940s. $75-$125.

86 World War II: 1940s

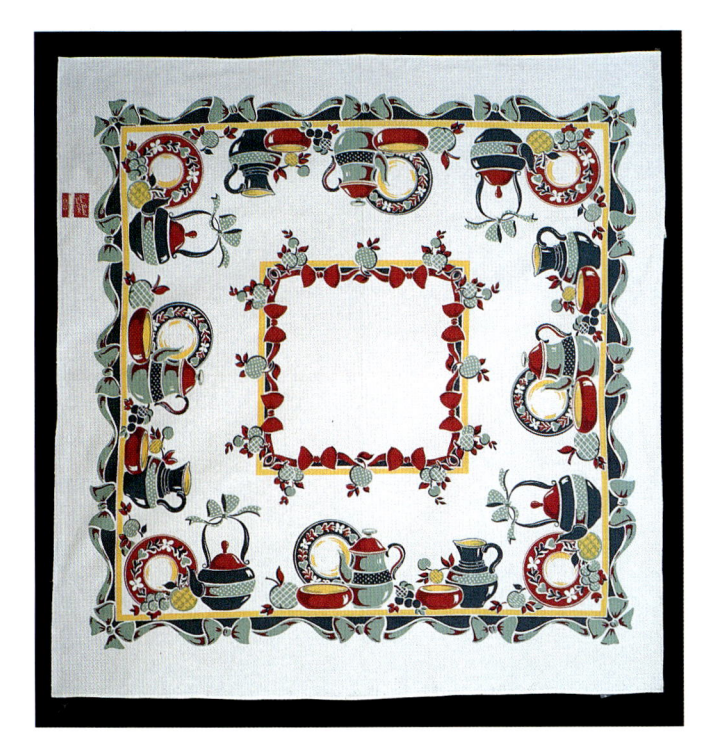

Mint Broderie Creations "Teapot and Bows" tablecloth. Delightful fiesta colored tablecloth. A definite show stopper for tea parties and luncheons, late 1940s. $100-$150.

Broderie Creations tag.

Detail of "Lady of the House" graphics.

Whimsical "Lady of the House" tablecloth. Delightful graphics and colors, most likely a "JS&S" tablecloth, late 1940s. My absolute favorite. $150-$175.

More detail of "Lady of the House" graphics.

World War II: 1940s 87

Wild west theme with Indians on horseback. Feedsack breakfast tablecloth, 1940s. $25-$45.

Wonderful thematic "Hard Times" tablecloth depicting a couple through their lives. Great graphics, late 1940s. $75-$95.

Darling "fantasia" flower fairies dance around orange clusters, early 1940s. $100-$125.

Close-up of fantasia fairies.

88 World War II: 1940s

Mint Startex "Roy Rogers" tablecloth. Bold colors and great graphics make this a favorite of collectors, early 1940s. $225-$350.

Startex tag.

Pennsylvania Dutch inspired yummy "Feast" tablecloth, late 1940s. $50-$75.

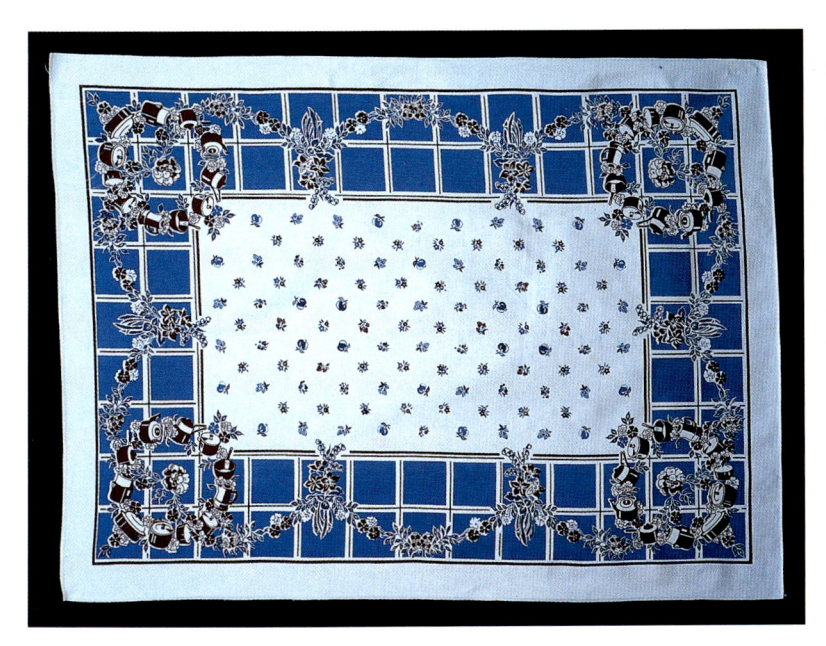

Fun kitchen pots and pans mixed with florals make this a whimsical treasure, late 1940s. $75-$100.

World War II: 1940s   89

Desert resort theme, beautiful cactus and palm trees and a hidden hotel decorate this unusual tablecloth, 1940s. $60-$85.

Mint Rosemary Products "Mexican pottery" tablecloth, early 1940s. $75-$95.

Simtex "Blue Willow" patterned tablecloth. Also came in red, late 1940s. $75-$95.

Feedsack tablecloth. Wonderful scattered Mexican theme, early 1940s. $45-$55.

90   World War II: 1940s

Mint Condition Simtex "Pueblo" tablecloth. Stunning fiesta colors, 1940s. An advertisement featuring this tablecloth is shown on page 49. $150-$175.

Simtex "Pueblo" tag.

Wilendur "fiesta pottery" tablecloth. Fun colors, late 1940s. $50-$75.

Repeating Mexican themed home yard goods tablecloth. Note the uneven hem, early 1940s. $45-$75.

World War II: 1940s 91

Muted pinks and blue Mexican tablecloth, but not an ordinary one. Note the 1940s styled woman in each corner, late 1940s. $75-$100.

Detail of the 1940s Mexican woman tablecloth.

Mint Exclusive brand Mexican themed tablecloth. Bold fabulous graphics, late 1940s. $50-$75.

Exclusive tag.

92 World War II: 1940s

Mexican pottery and floral arrangement in soft pinks, blues, and yellows, early 1940s. $50-$75.

Spanish bullfighter tablecloth. Wonderful graphics, late 1940s. $50-$75.

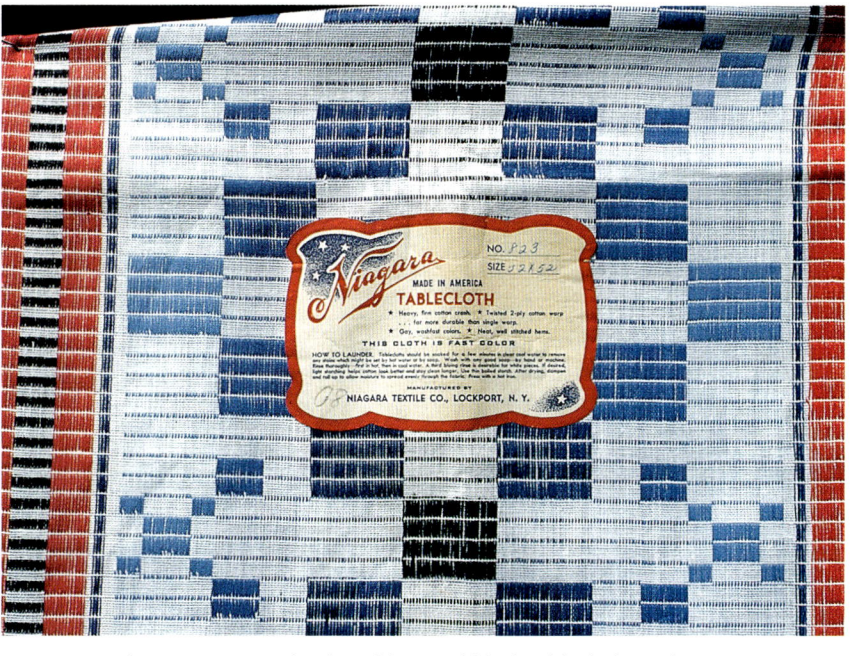

Niagara Textile Co. woven red, white, blue, and black tablecloth, early 1940s. The Niagara Falls area had many textile manufacturing plants that used hydropower machinery from the late 1800s to the 1940s. $50-$75.

World War II: 1940s 93

Soft cotton faded California state tablecloth, early 1940s. $40-$75.

Startex Starfield tag.

Mint Startex Starfield. Repeating pattern of Pennsylvania Dutch inspired florals, late 1940s. $55-$75.

94   World War II: 1940s

Chapter 8
Prosperity: 1950s

When the 1940s ended and the 1950s began, America was entering a prosperous time in history. It was a decade filled with much enthusiasm as Americans looked towards a more optimistic future. This is reflected in the excitement and exuberance of tablecloth designs from this era. The decade was a time of enormous growth, energy, and variety. Many cultural and political movements that would explode on the American scene in the 1960s were already gathering momentum during the '50s. With the end of World War II, American culture was primed for growth and change in nearly every area of fashion, politics, and consumerism.

As the 1950s continued, the average American lifestyle improved steadily. The "affordable tract home" was slowly taking over the rural farmlands and countryside, spreading the populations of urban cities beyond their former boundaries. People benefited from this period of expansion and development in industry and trade, and more money was now available for all kinds of consumer goods. After years of rationing for almost everything during the war, Americans were in the mood for lavish designs, coordinating kitchen textile fabrics, and easy care tablecloths. Manufacturers responded with witty, fun, and sometimes surreal designs.

Many people could now afford a new home. With Americans' renewed financial prosperity they liked to show off their wealth and possessions, much like the earlier Victorians. Food and alcohol seemed to be popular themes in 1950s tablecloth design, exemplifying the "good life." Neighborhood barbecues, cocktail parties, and other social gathering were popular ways to entertain with fanciful tablecloths depicting quirky themes. Tablecloth designers responded with designs that featured household items like bowls, teapots, and glassware all artfully arranged around the tablecloth. They also pictured quaint home interiors — hearths, living rooms, and kitchens. Whimsical garden themes with an abundance of fruits and vegetables and jubilant farmers were also fashionable.

Circus and children's themes were also very popular, influenced by Disney's release of *Dumbo*. Artist Grandma Moses influenced the simplistic folk and farm designs that appeared in abundance during this period. Western, cowboy, colonial, and Pennsylvania Dutch designs were also popular in the 1950s and can be found in abundance in the vintage tablecloth market today.

Following World War II, a number of factors combined to foster a new direction in home products and textiles. Designers like Verner Panton and Charles and Ray Eames responded to the new open plan architecture of the modern home with furnishings that were seen as functional "free standing art forms." Kitchen textiles were designed with bold geometric and abstract free form shapes and textures. 1950s tablecloth manufacturers like "Styled by Dervan" featured motifs by prominent textile designers of the time, each with a different style and flavor and always with the artists' signature in the corner of the tablecloth. These are wacky, fun, stylistic examples of what was popular during the 1950s.

A prominent designer, Russel Wright, created new broad loomed plaids to coordinate with his china dinnerware patterns. Tablecloths were also produced specifically for use with 1940s and 1950s china patterns such as "Blue Willow" and Hall's "Autumn Leaf," as well as other patterns of family china. These were a refreshing change to the white damasks, sweet berries, and bright floral printed cotton tablecloths that had defined 1940s tablecloth patterns.

Americans broke away from traditional prints and designs and looked for modern, space age stylized kitchen textiles to coordinate with their Swedish/Danish modern furniture and sleek vinyl and chrome tabletops. The 1950s brought more man-made fabrics such as Banlon, Orlon, polyester, and acrylics. These "space age" fabrics were easy care, crease resistant, kept their shape and dried quickly. This fit in with the popular low maintenance lifestyle that was portrayed by advertisers targeting the modern housewife. Many tablecloths from this era were promoted with an emphasis on such features: "Party flair with simple fare," "No fussing with to serve an unexpected guest," and "Easy laundering and budget priced."

At the end of the 1950s, tablecloth manufacturers began incorporating metallic gold overlay into their prints. Unfortunately, this technique was not always colorfast and the gold was the first to fade. Designers also used metallic threads woven into the cloth to provide sparkle, dimension, and sensory delight. In 1958, mandatory labels were required to be sewn in tablecloths stating fiber content and also the percentage of fiber by weight, such as "80% cotton, 20% rayon." The label also had to list the manufacturer name and location. Many popular vintage tablecloths can be dated using this as a reference guide. Both the paper "store labels" and sewn in tags have this expanded information.

Bright, fun, colorful, and exciting patterns made their way onto everything conceivable. The only limitation to these wonderfully appealing designs was imagination. Imagery was drawn from a great variety of social and political influences of the time. The popularity of the "Black Americana" and "Mammy" themed tablecloths were an example of this. These were popular in the 1950s when the social injustices perpetrated on black Americans were brought to our attention by charismatic social leader Dr Martin Luther King. These tablecloths are collected now, by some, as a reminder of the past — an example of how far we have come as Americans.

When most people think of the '50s, they think "kitsch" — items that can be flamboyant in their design, but have a fun appeal to them. The attraction of the 1950s for the tablecloth collector is the sheer variety of fun patterns and bold prints that were available during this prosperous time in America's textile history.

Simtex advertisement showing a checkered tweed tablecloth. *With permission from WestPoint Stevens Inc.*

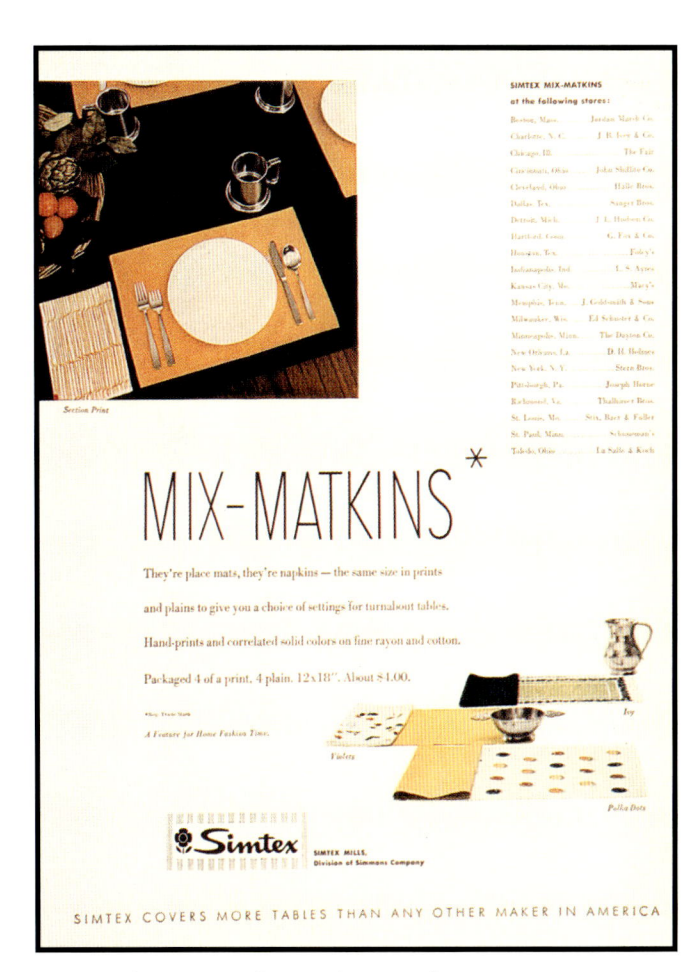

Simtex advertisement for "Matkins." *With permission from WestPoint Stevens Inc.*

Simtex advertisement promoting Russel Wright designs. *With permission from WestPoint Stevens Inc.*

"Springtime Dress For Your Table." *With permission from WestPoint Stevens Inc.*

Prosperity: 1950s 97

Simtex advertisement for Weavecraft, featuring a barbecue scene. *With permission from WestPoint Stevens Inc.*

Simtex advertisement showing "Cross-stitch" tablecloth. *With permission from WestPoint Stevens Inc.*

Simtex advertisement for Candlelight damask. *With permission from WestPoint Stevens Inc.*

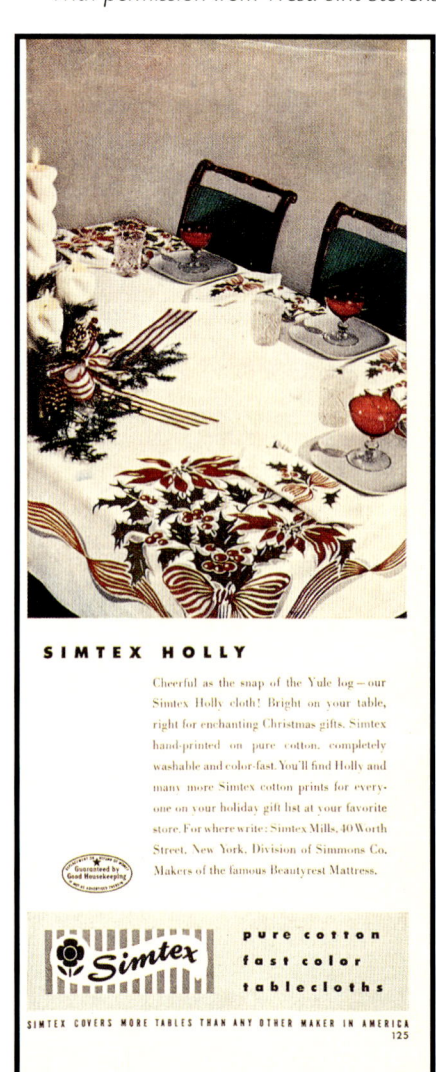

Simtex Christmas advertisement. *With permission from WestPoint Stevens Inc.*

98   Prosperity: 1950s

Left:
Simtex advertisement for leaf print tablecloth. *With permission from WestPoint Stevens Inc.*

Right:
Simtex advertisement showing gift packaged tablecloth sets. *With permission from WestPoint Stevens Inc.*

Martex advertisement. *With permission from WestPoint Stevens Inc.*

Simtex advertisement featuring "Exotic" pattern tablecloth. *With permission from WestPoint Stevens Inc.*

Prosperity: 1950s 99

Leacock boxed "Spring Glow" tablecloth napkin set, 1950s. $75-$150.

Mint Leacock "Autumn Glow" tablecloth. A profusion of fall colors, early 1950s. $65-$75.

Leacock Quality Hand Prints tag.

100 Prosperity: 1950s

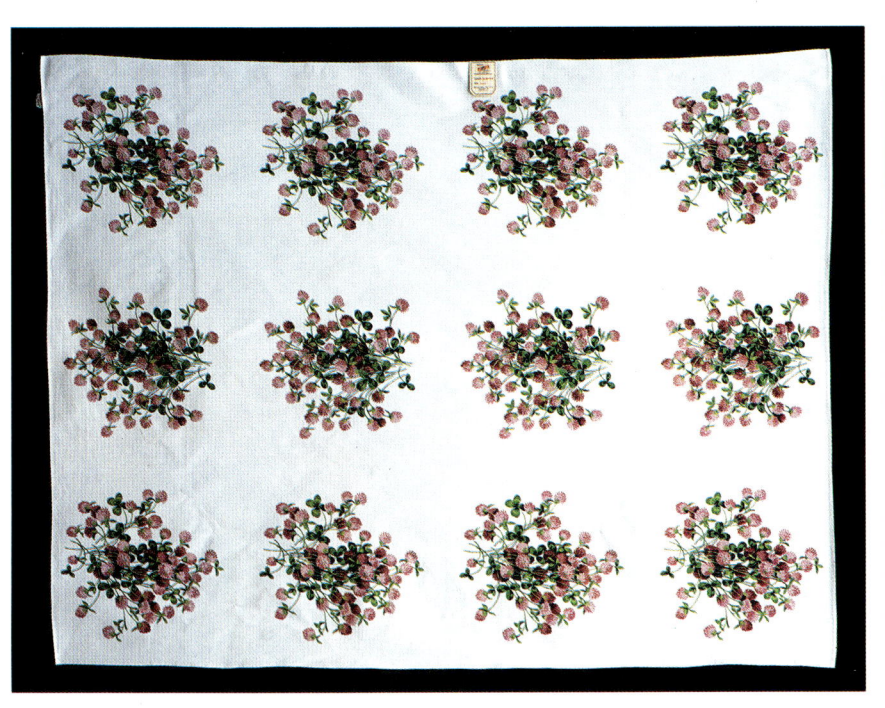

Wilendur "Clover" tag.

Mint Wilendur "Clover" patterned tablecloth, a harder to find design, classic Wilendur repeating pattern, early 1950s. $75-$125.

Simtex/Stevens produced this dramatic blue rose tablecloth shortly after they merged, late 1950s $50-$75.

Stevens Hand Prints. Brown florals make a wonderful fall tablecloth, late 1950s. $50-$75.

Prosperity: 1950s 101

Pennsylvania Dutch inspired 1950s floral and chickens tablecloth. $50-$75.

Detail of Pennsylvania Dutch inspired brown floral and chickens tablecloth.

Late 1950s abundant florals create a warm inviting tablecloth. $45-$55.

Simtex Stevens bold green roses cover this late 1950s tablecloth. $40-$50.

102   Prosperity: 1950s

Pennsylvania Dutch themed tulip tablecloth, 1950s. $40-$50.

Lovely red floral set against a red and gray geometric pattern, early 1950s. $45-$55.

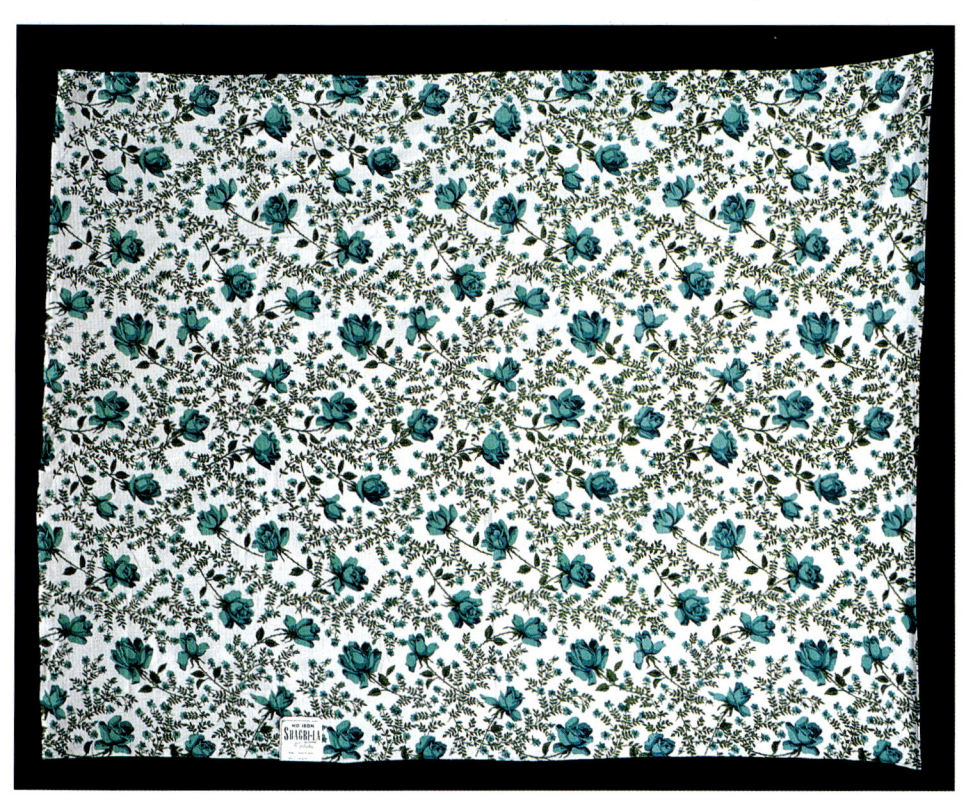

Wilendure "Shaggy Rose" tablecloth. Nubby cotton with chintz blue rose design, late 1950s. $50-$75.

Wilendure Shagri-la tag. Note the "e" at the end, which dates this to after 1958.

Prosperity: 1950s   103

Leacock Quality Hand Prints tag.

Mint Leacock "Wild Rose" tablecloth, cool tones with gold metallic accents, late 1950s. $45-$50.

Soft pink and brown linen tablecloth. Pennsylvania Dutch influenced floral pattern, early 1950s. $50-$75.

Soft pink and gray flowing romantic flora, early 1950s. $50-$75.

104　Prosperity: 1950s

The 1950s oriental influence is evident in this green, cherry blossom branch themed tablecloth. $50-$75.

Hardy Craft oriental inspired floral and bird design, early 1950s. $45-$55.

Vera signature without the "ladybug" design.

Vera screen printed "Daffodils" tablecloth. Rich, vivid colors in cool tones, early 1950s. $75-$125.

Prosperity: 1950s

Startex "Daisy" tablecloth. Vivid spring colors, early 1950s. $60-$75.

Pale gray roses and butterflies outlined in black, a characteristic of late 1950s tablecloths. $45-$55.

Mint JS&S and Parisian Prints poppy and daisy print tablecloth. Signed "Paris" in corner. $75-$150.

JS&S Prints and Parisian Prints tags on the same tablecloth. It could be JS&S was the importer or the name of a store.

106   **Prosperity: 1950s**

Mint Kempray K&B "Rambler Rose" tablecloth. A blue rose garland in geometric pattern, early 1950s. $50-$75.

Kempray K&B Hand Prints tag.

Unusual red and black leaf patterned tablecloth. Bold and beautiful, early 1950s. $50-$75.

Morning glories and roses frame a bright yellow tablecloth from the early 1950s. $50-$65.

Prosperity: 1950s 107

Cool blue poppies surround this wonderful late 1950s tablecloth. $50-$65.

Bold maroon and pale blue florals and ribbons. Gorgeous tablecloth, early 1950s. $50-$75.

Startex "Autumn Leaf" tablecloth to coordinate with Hall china pattern of the same name, 1950s. $95-$150.

Wrought iron, greenery and candles. A very 1950s design. $50-$65.

Mint Hardy Craft "Leaves" tablecloth. Scattered multi-colored leaves give this tablecloth a wonderful fall feel, early 1950s. $55-$75.

Hardy Craft tag.

Mint California Hand Prints "Moon Flower" tablecloth, Rayon, early 1950s. $50-$75.

Prosperity: 1950s 109

Lush deep red rayon tablecloth with yellow roses, late 1950s design. $50-$65.

Large corner groupings of gray and pink flowers, cool elegance, late 1950s. $50-$75.

Sweet spring floral bouquets in a delicately patterned tablecloth, early 1950s. $45-$55.

Interesting wrought iron, greenery and candles. Also came in red. $45-$60.

Hand block printed fruit tablecloth, late 1950s. $40-$50.

California Hand Prints, tropical flowers in soft browns, pinks, and greens, early 1950s. $50-$75.

Delightful pink roses and a subtle polka dot center by JS&S, 1950s. $50-$75.

JS&S tag.

Prosperity: 1950s 111

1950s maroon and cinnamon colored daisy tablecloth. $45-$65.

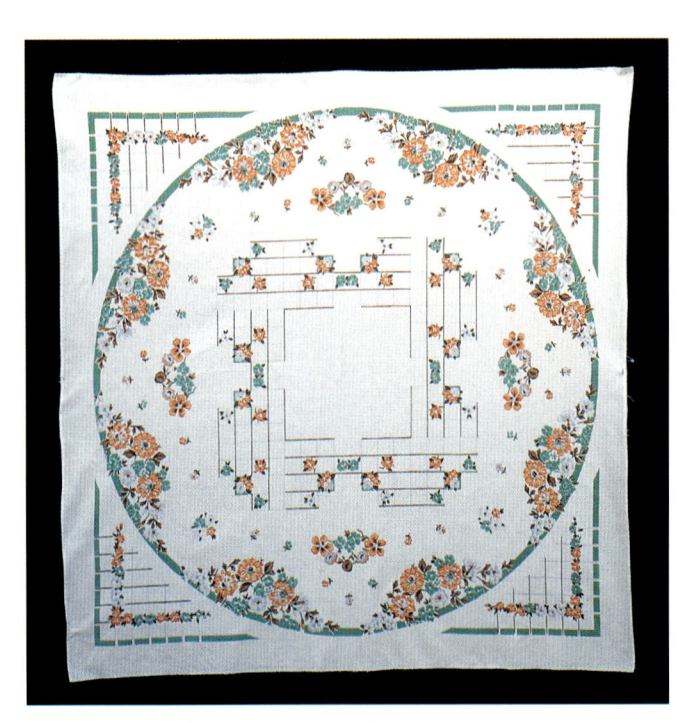

Geometric floral pattern in browns and green, early 1950s. $50-$75.

Pale yellow and white floral tablecloth, late 1950s. $40-$50.

Blue and maroon flowers with a geometric edge make this a sweet soft summer evening party tablecloth, early 1950s. $75-$100.

Soft strawberries and tulips decorate this early 1950s tablecloth. $35-$45.

Cheerful yellow checks and abundant fruits to brighten any winter kitchen, late 1950s. J.C. Penney Pennicraft label. *From the collection of Sonja Gibson.* $40-$50.

Rosemary Products flower mark.

Brown chilis and dried corn make an interesting southwest themed tablecloth. Rosemary Products, with "flower" logo, late 1950s. $45-$65.

Prosperity: 1950s   113

Fall colors and tole painted coffee pots make this a visually interesting design, late 1950s $45-$55.

Bountiful baskets of fresh picked vegetables, a favorite theme of post war designers, early 1950s. $95-$125.

Succulent grapefruit and sweet dogwoods make a darling brunch cloth, early 1950s. $50-$75.

Wonderful bright kitchen tablecloth. This makes a great BBQ tablecloth, late 1950s. $50-$75.

114 Prosperity: 1950s

Mauve one color fruits grace this warm, inviting tablecloth, early 1950s. $50-$75.

Pineapple and floral tablecloth with warm yellow tones, early 1950s. $35-$55.

Mint Falflax pure linen "Minton" design tablecloth. Pinks and grays, strawberries and floral, late 1950s. $50-$75.

Falflax pure linen tag.

Prosperity: 1950s   115

Themes of kitchen utensils, spices, and vegetables make a darling 1950s tablecloth. $45-$50.

Soft pink, brown, and yellow floral and pinecones design, late 1940s. $50-$75.

Blue fruit, baskets, and bows. A wonderful fall tablecloth, early 1950s. $60-$75.

Sweet berries in a repeating pattern, most likely a Weil & Durrse manufactured tablecloth, early 1950s. $75-$95.

Fabulous fall colors in a fruit and vegetable tablecloth, late 1950s. $45-$55.

Sweet cherries and gold flowers makes a darling summer cloth, early 1950s. $65-$75.

Linen "Apple" tablecloth. A delightful design, 1950s. *From the collection of Pearl Yeadon*. $55-$75.

Colorful folk figures dance around the edge of this linen tablecloth, early 1950s. $50-$75.

Prosperity: 1950s 117

Darling farm children tablecloth. This one is produced by Leacock Prints and is their "Sweetheart" pattern. I love the polka dot accents, early 1940s. $75-$85.

Pennsylvania Dutch themed "Folk" tablecloth manufactured by Parisian Prints, early 1950s. $45-$65.

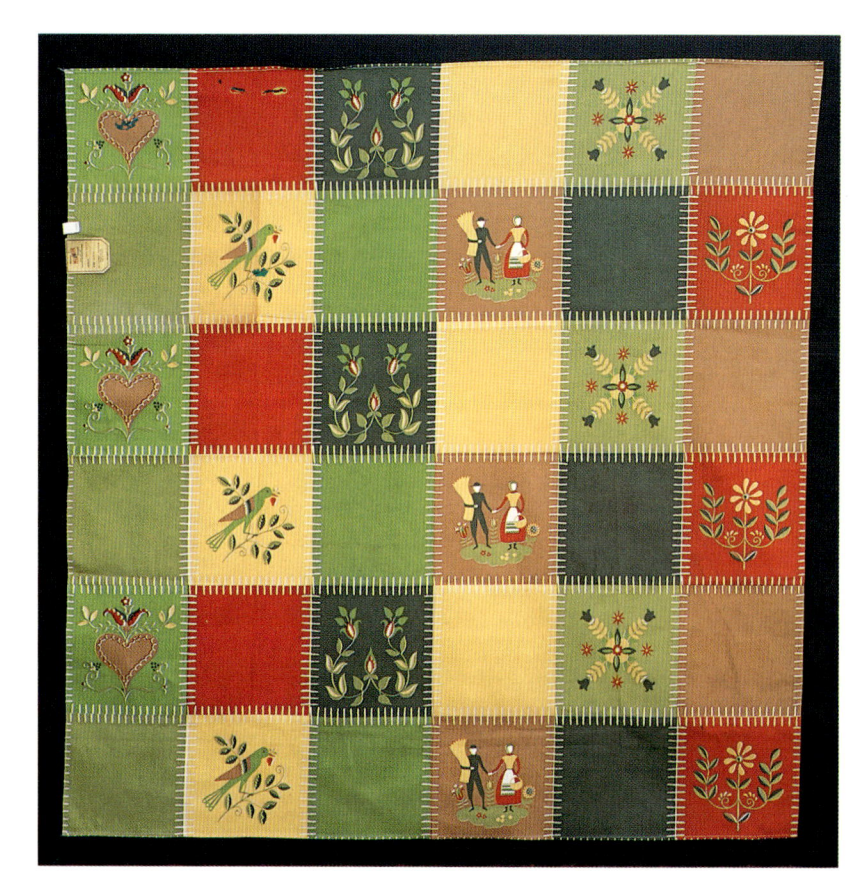

Mint Wilendur "Penn-Dutch" patterned tablecloth. A warm quilt-like design, early 1950s. $75-$125.

Wilendur "Penn-Dutch" tag.

118   Prosperity: 1950s

Colonial revival themes in a vividly colored tablecloth, early 1950s. $50-$75.

Darling Pennsylvania Dutch style "stitched" chickens and flowers theme, late 1950s. $50-$60.

Red and black geometric and floral pattern, so characteristic of the 1950s prints. $40-$50.

Stylized tulips in well ordered grid pattern, 1950s. $40-$65.

Prosperity: 1950s 119

Pale blue cups and spoons decorated with little roosters. Roosters and chickens were popular 1950s themes. $45-$60.

Colonial revival and art deco motifs create an elegant tablecloth, early 1950s. $50-$75.

Mint Bucilla "Folklore" kitchen coordinating set: blender cover, toaster cover, hot pads, and tablecloth. Many other accessories were available in this collection, early 1950s. $45-$125.

Bucilla "Folklore" tag.

120   Prosperity: 1950s

"Happy Hostess" linen tablecloth. Darling graphics and poem, most likely a Bucilla tablecloth. It was made to be cross stitched, but collectors like it this way. Early 1950s. $65-$75.

Colonial revival influenced tablecloth. "x-stitched" pattern used most often by the Bucilla Company, early 1950s. $50-$75.

Mint Garden State "Sampler" tablecloth. Interesting themes of home and horses, late 1950s. $55-$75.

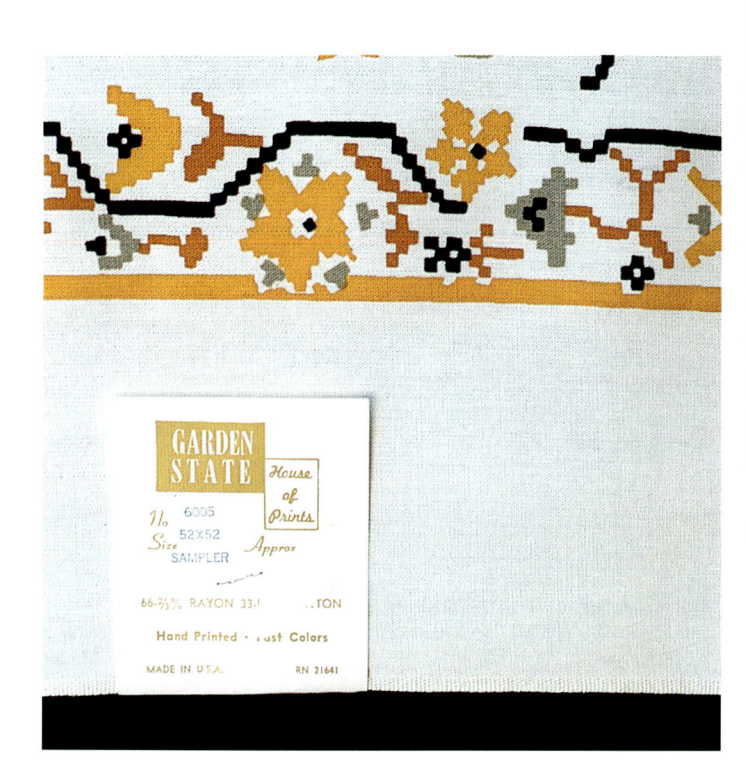

Garden State House of Prints tag.

Prosperity: 1950s 121

"Bless this house" Colonial America themed tablecloth, early 1950s. $75-$100.

Colonial revival influenced tablecloth with scenes of the "good ole days," early 1950s. $50-$75.

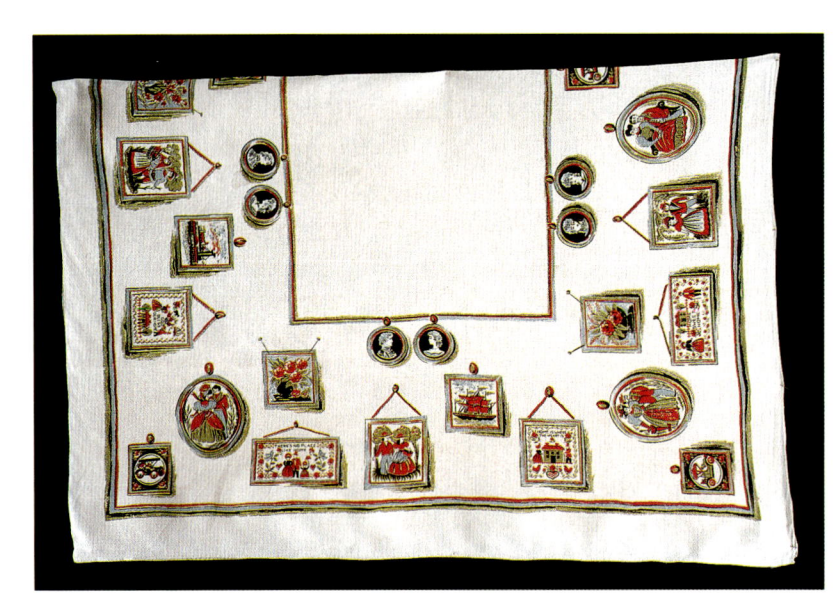

Themes of "Home Sweet Home" and colonial influence make this an interesting tablecloth, early 1950s. $50-$75.

Mint cream damask tablecloth and napkins. "Damask Superior" made in occupied Japan, 1950s. $50-$75.

122   Prosperity: 1950s

Florida 1950s tablecloth. Flamingos and hibiscus themes make this a darling of collectors. $75-$125.

Wonderful "Lake Michigan" tablecloth. An example of souvenir tablecloths that feature tourist attractions, early 1950s. $100-$150.

Alaska state tablecloth. The discovery of oil in 1957 pushed Alaska into statehood in 1959; since there is no indication of statehood and there are oil wells depicted, we can date this to between 1957 and 1959. $50-$75.

Montana state tablecloth, great bold western graphics, 1950s. $150-$200.

Prosperity: 1950s 123

Unusual western states souvenir tablecloth. This one is damaged, late 1950s. $45-$100.

Mint California Hand Prints "Desert Poppy" rust colored tablecloth. Advertised to coordinate with classic dinnerware. Rayon, 1950s. $75-$125.

Yucca Prints label.

Mint Yucca Print "California" tablecloth. Bold colors and fun graphics make this a collector's favorite, early 1950s. $75-$95.

124   Prosperity: 1950s

Floral garlands and elegant ribbons give this early 1950s tablecloth a geometric influence. $60-$85.

Surreal trees and scattered florals make this a visually interesting tablecloth, early 1950s. $50-$75.

Simtex cool browns, teal, and gold. These are classic 1950s colors to coordinate with the "Mod" china patterns. $40-$50.

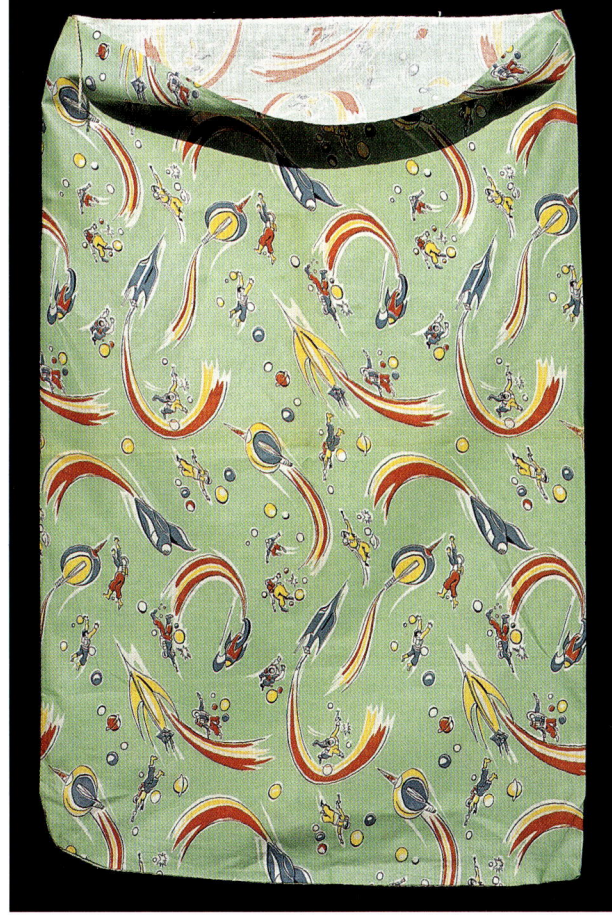

Unused space themed feedsack. This one is still sewn up as a "bag"; it would be used for many household items, like tablecloths, early 1950s. $100-$125.

Prosperity: 1950s

Simtex "X Ranch" tablecloth. Dude ranches were very popular as vacation destinations in the late 1940s and early 1950s. Early 1950s. $75-$125.

Small polka dot and roses bridge cloth, manufactured by Corticelli, early 1950s. $40-$55.

Startex cowboy themed tablecloth. This one has it all: cowboys, steer, cactus and guns, early 1950s. $100-$150.

Linen floral tablecloth with geometric influences, early 1950s. $45-$55.

126 Prosperity: 1950s

Simtex simple kitchen plaid, early 1950s. $45-$60.

Teal and orange floral geometric designed tablecloth, early 1950s. $45-$55.

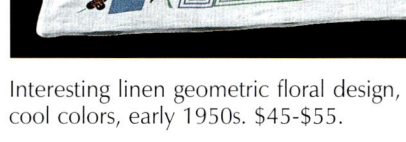

Interesting linen geometric floral design, cool colors, early 1950s. $45-$55.

Plaid tablecloth by Simtex, possibly a "Russel Wright," early 1950s. $45-$125.

Prosperity: 1950s 127

JS&S tag.

Mint JS&S manufactured windowpane geometric pattern. This same pattern is available in green, early 1950s. $65-$80.

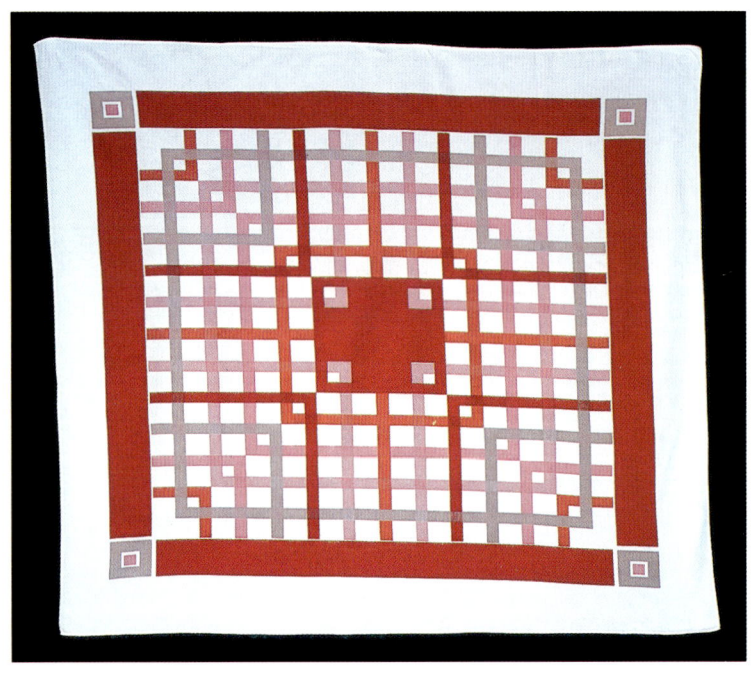

Geometric pattern of pink and red to coordinate with the Danish modern kitchen, early 1950s. $50-$75.

JS&S manufactured windowpane geometric pattern, 1950s. The rope edge gives it an elegant "deco" feel. $65-$80.

Geometric designs were favorites of 1950s designers. $50-$75.

Simtex bold geometric pattern, early 1950s. $40-$50.

Geometric concentric patterns of bright squares, Verner Panton influenced design, early 1950s. *From the collection of George McGinnis.* $65-$85.

California Hand Prints, fountains and tropical fauna in stunning rich color, late 1950s. $50-$75.

Prosperity: 1950s 129

Beautiful gold tablecloth with white and pink cherry blossoms, early 1950s. $50-$60.

Late 1950s delicate oriental themed tablecloth in pink and blue. $50-$75.

Soft browns and sweet florals. Another one of my grandmother's tablecloths, late 1950s. $45-$55.

Stunning use of bold colors in this oriental themed floral tablecloth, late 1950s. $55-$75.

130   Prosperity: 1950s

Mint Simtex Stevens "Little Angel" tablecloth, with gold metallic accents and great late 1950s graphics. $125-$175.

Simtex/Stevens "Little Angel" tag.

1950s Christmas theme with pine garlands and bright ornaments. $60-$75.

Close-up of the little angels.

Prosperity: 1950s   131

Gypsies dance around this delightful 1950s tablecloth. $50-$75.

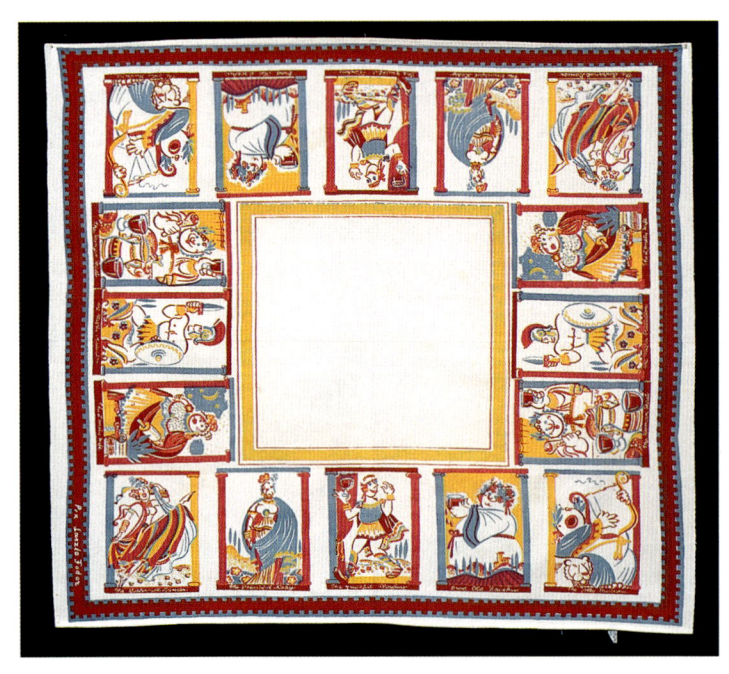

Whimsical farmer and wife tablecloth. Darling graphics, early 1950s. $75-$125.

Styled by Dervan, 1950s designer signed printed tablecloth. This one is "Greek Players" by Lazlo Fodor, 1950s. $50-$75.

Styled by Dervan label.

132   Prosperity: 1950s

Pickwick Tavern Dickens tablecloth, with themes from Dickens's novel *The Pickwick Papers*, early 1950s. $50-$75.

Red gingham and animals make a darling summer barbecue tablecloth. Designed by Carrie Wilson, early 1950s. $50-$75.

Mint Table Tempo linen tablecloth, "Hummel style" children, early 1950s. $45-75.

Table Tempo tag.

Prosperity: 1950s 133

Simtex "Gold Rush" western tablecloth. Boom town graphics, amazing detail, early 1950s. *From the collection of DeDe G. Ford.* $175-$300.

Detail of "Gold Rush" tablecloth.

Mint "Prints Du Jour" tablecloth imported from Japan tablecloth. Blue chickens and birds done in "mod" style, early 1950s. $60-$75.

Prints du Jour tag.

134 Prosperity: 1950s

Mint Leacock Quality Hand Prints tablecloth with a southern plantation and cottage roses design. $75-$95.

Tag for Leacock Quality Hand Prints Redi-set by Northern.

Hardy Craft "farm" linen tablecloth. Wonderful depiction of Grandma Moses inspired themes of farms, animals, and crops, early 1950s. $75-$125.

Farm house tablecloth by Hardy Craft. Popular farm and homestead themes were frequently found on early 1950s tablecloths. $45-$65.

Prosperity: 1950s

A wonderful Christmas tablecloth, most likely a "Parisian Prints," late 1950s. $35-$50.

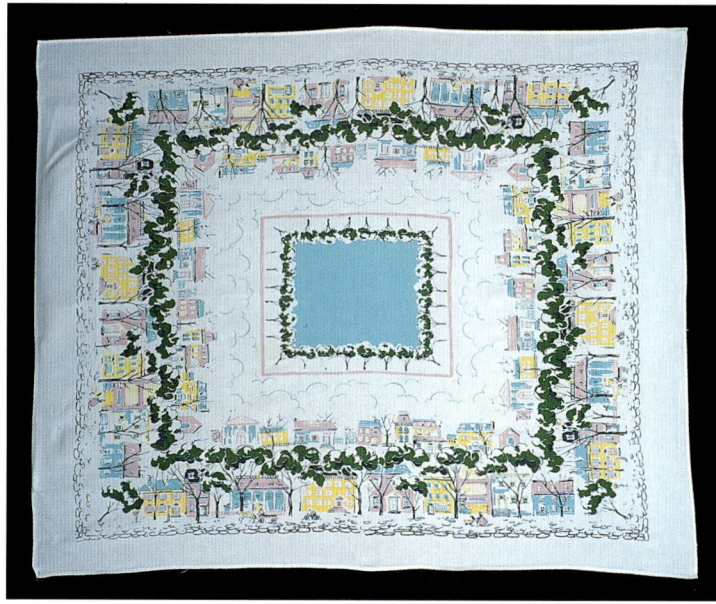

Cobblestone street tablecloth, early Victorian influenced themes in 1950s colors. $55-$75.

Sweet little fairy children and bunnies dance in the garden. Made by "Dunmoy," an Irish import, early 1950s. $50-$75.

Dunmoy tag.

136   **Prosperity: 1950s**

Chickens and kitchen accessories make this an interesting tablecloth from the early 1950s. $25-$50.

Pink linen Florida map tablecloth. The Florida map is almost completely faded, late 1950s. $45-$125.

Kitchen utensils and spices, very popular 1950s themes. $50-$75.

Prosperity: 1950s 137

Mint Parisian Prints "Vermont" tablecloth with kitchen utensil theme, early 1950s. $65-$80.

Mint Fairfield tablecloth, blues and greens, late 1950s. $25-$50.

Sweet shop linen tablecloth, another "good life" 1950s theme. $25-$50.

Only in the 1950s could you have a lime, gold, and pink color combination in a tablecloth. Darling classic "kitchen items" theme. I love this one. $50-$75.

1950s kitchen theme condiment cloth. Interesting details and colors. $40-$50.

Tole painted kitchenware and cigar store Indians make an interesting tablecloth, early 1950s. $45-$60.

Mint SunGlo "Vegetable Salad" tablecloth. The table's set for a feast, early 1950s. $40-$55.

SunGlo tag.

Prosperity: 1950s 139

Blues and browns kitchen themed tablecloth. "Lucy and Ricky" would be proud to have this, late 1950s. $50-$75.

Country fair theme in blues and golds, a cute late 1950s tablecloth. $50-$75.

Wilendure "Lobster" themed tablecloth. Repeating patterns of lobster, parsley, and clams make this a popular summer tablecloth. It came in small to very large sizes for the banquet table, early 1950s. $50-$95.

Rare "Fairy garden" tablecloth, fairies play and dance in a stylized floral garden complete with spider webs, delightful fall colors. 1950s. *From the collection of Pearl Yeadon.* $100-$125.

Chapter 9
Dating Tablecloths

Overview

Tablecloth design, like any other fashion art form, must reflect existing tastes and styles of the period to find a market. We can use the records of these fashions and moods to generally determine dates. Although in some cases the tablecloths can be assigned to a general decade, as I have done, or even to a specific group of years, the lack of manufacturing records or other cataloguing of these delightful keepsakes makes assigning any one date extremely difficult. For example, many tablecloth patterns were continuously fashionable and were available to the consumer for many years. Some popular fruit patterns were produced from the 1930s up until the late 1950s. There are, however, many clues to assist in the dating of tablecloths, which can be found through a study of period fabric, designs, colors, and styles.

Just as fashions changed and evolved thorough the decades, so did the styles of the vintage tablecloth. Certain patterns and fabrics enjoyed popularity during specific times. For example, flax table linens were usually homespun and only really produced up until the 1890s. Tablecloths made of 100% linen were fashionable up until the late 1930s, then cotton rayon blends were introduced and enjoyed popularity for their easy care properties. After the 1940s, you will find the same pattern of tablecloths offered in many different choices of fabrics, like cotton, linen and rayon blends, as well as in many color variations.

The search for specific production dates, qualification of types of fabrics used, as well as an investigation into the dying/printing process has been one of the most delightful and rewarding challenges of categorizing of my own collection. This pursuit has resulted in the information and guidelines that follow, which should help you in dating your own vintage tablecloths. In some cases, I have used the information that was available to make an estimation or "best guess" in dating the tablecloths illustrated in this book.

As will be seen, identifying the dyeing and printing process used to decorate a tablecloth is one way of dating the piece. These processes have changed dramatically during the last hundred years as new equipment and dyes were invented and improved. The information was so interesting, I have included separate chapters on the "History of Dyes," and "Types of Printing."

We cannot draw complete parallels between vintage dress goods fabrics and household table linen productions. Tablecloths were produced to be inexpensive goods; they were printed quickly and usually with simple printing processes. When it became easier in the 1930s to produce dress fabrics with as many as twelve colors, household tablecloths were being produced in two or three color combinations.

Most tablecloths with signs of fugitive dyes indicate a pre-1935 date, although you will also find fugitive dyes appearing in tablecloths that were produced during World War II when good quality dyes were scarce. Over dyed patterns, along with a count of the number of colors used in the pattern, will help you determine the approximate age of your tablecloth. If the tablecloth contains a tag or paper label, there is a wealth of information at your fingertips and you will be better able to identify the period of manufacture. Government regulations changed the information required on these tags, and certain dated terms were used to give the consumer greater confidence in the tablecloth, such as "Fast Colors" and "Sanforized." For quick reference, there is a list at the end of this chapter which summarizes the clues you may use to date your tablecloth.

It's fun to assemble a collection spanning the hundred or more years of tablecloth production and design. A wonderful, heavy 1890s Turkey Red Victorian fringed damask, several 1930s faded fruit and gray leaf tablecloths, many 1940s floral printed tablecloths, and quirky 1950s "space age" geometric shaped tablecloths all have a place of honor in my vintage printed tablecloth collection.

History of Dyes

It is interesting to note that the early settlement of America by the English was in part a push to acquire the abundant native resources of this new land. Prior to the colonization of America, natural dyes had to be shipped from the "Far East" at great expense. Natural sources of dyes in the Americas, such as cochineal, logwood, madder, and indigo, gave the early colonists raw materials that possessed great economic value to the English.

In the mid 1700s, the craft of bleaching and dyeing depended on the skill gained by a lengthy apprenticeship for a male specialist. The manufacture of natural dyes required a good deal of skill and knowledge of biology, especially when using the more complicated dyes like indigo. Indigo blue was produced through a long process of controlled fermentation over a number of days. The bleaching and dying processes were complex, difficult to control, and in the case of exotic colors, expensive to produce.

The household dyeing of textiles by women flourished in Colonial America, made possible by the availability of a range of natural dyestuffs that the colonists learned about from native peoples. The colonists themselves discovered the excellent brown shades that came from black walnut hulls as well as the yellows that came from the bark of the American black oak.

By the early 1800s, published formulas for a number of dyes were available to the craftsman and the home dyer. However, there were distinct differences between the two. All professional craft dyers were men during this time. They represented the commercial economic world and sought to maintain control of their trade secrets. Household dyers were women and their techniques were shared openly. Their household duties often included spinning thread and weaving cloth for their families and it was only natural that they dyed the material with dyestuffs they made from the materials at hand — and shared that information with other women.

Mechanization and the factory system of production, following the Industrial Revolution, were incorporated into the textile industry. The discovery of chlorine in the early 1800s speeded up the bleaching of textiles, so that while it used to take months in the eighteenth century to dye and bleach cloth, it could now be accomplished in hours by the late nineteenth century. The most significant advancement for artificial dyestuffs came in 1856, when William Perkins created a synthetic purple dye from coal tar. Perkins called this new dye color "mauve."

By the late 1890s, Germany had discovered synthetic dyes, which gave them a competitive advantage and eventual domination of the dyestuffs industry. German chemists soon developed new ranges of colors and also learned to synthesize such popular natural dyestuffs as indigo and madder. Consequently, German scientific discoveries forced natural dyestuffs out of the commercial market, the profits from which then allowed Germany to branch out into pharmaceuticals and explosives just as the world was beginning to edge towards war. By 1914, Germany was producing about 85% of the world's supply of dyes and dyestuffs, and its trading partners were responsible for most of the rest. Since the connection between coal tar products and explosives was apparent, the U.S. government was concerned as well. American textile mills were unfortunately dependent on these dyes and they were ill prepared for what was to happen next: a dye embargo in 1914 with the advent of World War I.

The American synthetic dye industry was thus catapulted into existence by a sudden and dramatic government action on its own behalf as the "spoils" of war allowed for the seizing of German dye processes and patents. By the early 1920s, government sponsored agencies established the basis for creation of American dyestuffs and new dye manufacturing plants like Du Pont quickly stepped in to fill the void left by the dye embargo.

Example of World War II era unstable dyes. Note the pale purple "ghost" figure.

Example of unstable, fugitive dye — the darker blue dye has faded from the tablecloth on the right.

Dating Tablecloths 143

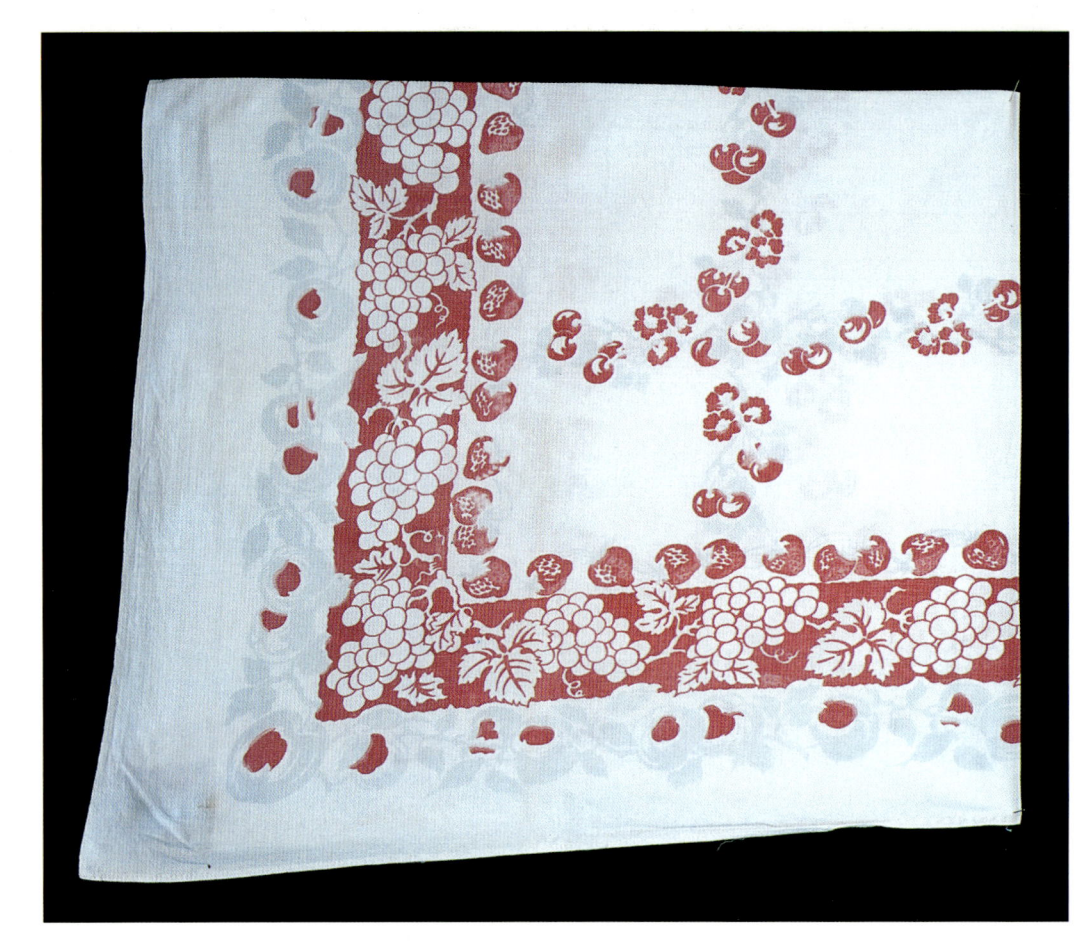

Another example of "fugitive dye" — a faint blue fruit pattern is evident in this tablecloth from the early 1930s.

Example of Perkins's "mauve" color on a Victorian felted table cover from the 1880s.

144 Dating Tablecloths

Trademark History

Throughout history, makers of goods have put their names or other marks on things they produce. Prior to the twentieth century, trademarks were usually symbols or pictures rather than words, since many people in the world could not read. As trade increased during the nineteenth century, many countries adopted laws recognizing the legal rights of trademark owners.

Congress passed the first federal trademark law in the United States in 1870. *The Trademark Act of 1920* was a revision of the first act of 1870. It was at this time that most tablecloth manufacturers registered their marks with the U.S. Government trademark office. The law prohibited other sellers from using similar marks that might confuse the public about the source of a product. The Trademark Act of 1946 (*The Lanham Act*) is administered by the U.S. Patent and Trademark Office (PTO). Trademark registration lasts for ten years but may be renewed indefinitely if the mark is still being used.

Mandatory Content and Performance Labels

Another useful tool in dating your tablecloths is to look for a sewn in tag or paper label. The *Textile Fiber Products Identification Act of 1958* mandated that a tag or label must list the name of the raw materials, fiber content, and percentage of fabrics by weight along with the manufacturer's address or registered identification number and county of origin. It must remain affixed (sewn into) the merchandise until it is sold. Finding this information on a label tells you that the item was produced after 1958.

The Federal Trade Commission mandated new regulations requiring that most home furnishings carry permanently attached labels giving care and maintenance information. Included in the requirements was how to wash tablecloths and whether they need to be dry cleaned or hung to dry. These tags were sewn into the tablecloths and will date them as post 1972.

Types of Printing Processes

Fabrics with colored designs are known as printed cloths. The printing of cloth represents an important part of the tablecloth manufacturing process. Early printed tablecloths were hand stamped simple designs, usually of a single color. As the printing process improved, more colors and increasingly elaborate designs were possible, allowing tablecloth designers to create more intricate and detailed designs. Identifying the printing process used on your tablecloth can be difficult, but if accomplished, this can be another useful tool for dating your tablecloth collection. Manufacturers used a variety of methods for printing fabrics. Some of them are explained below.

Hand Blocking

Before the method of direct roller printing was discovered, textiles were printed by hand. Hand blocking gave a greater variety of designs and color effects, as the regular repetition of a pattern that is necessary in the roller method is not necessary in hand blocking. A block of wood, copper, or other material bearing a design in relief with the dye paste applied to the surface is pressed on the fabric. Linen was the fabric of choice for hand blocking because it has the proper texture and quality to accept the dye. One way to detect hand blocking is to look along the selvage for the regularity of the design repetition. In roller printing, the design must be repeated at regular intervals. With hand blocking, one color runs into another in at least a few places, and the design may be uneven due to the "block" unevenly stamping the design across the tablecloth. This process is found most often in early homespun tablecloths prior to the 1850s and in "art pieces," created from approximately 1900 to the 1920s.

Example of a hand blocked tablecloth.

Direct or Copper Roller Printing

Developed in 1810, this is the simplest method and probably the most used up until the 1940s. The fabric was carried on a rotating central cylinder and pressed by a series of rollers each bearing one color. The design was engraved on the copper rollers by hand or machine pressure or etched by photoengraving methods. The color paste was applied to the rollers through feed rollers rotating in a color box. Earlier tablecloths were simple two color designs, but by the late 1930s, as many as eight colors could be printed very quickly.

Discharge Printing or Dyeing

With discharge printing, the whole cloth is dyed a solid color first, then the design on the roller is covered with a chemical which, when applied to the cloth, removes the color. This creates a pattern. Usually the pattern is lighter than the background color. This was used for some earlier printed cotton feedsack materials and textiles produced before the 1920s.

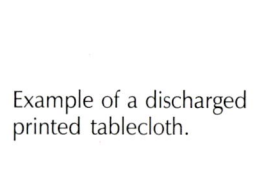

Example of a discharged printed tablecloth.

Resist Printing

In this method, the design is printed first with a chemical paste. The paste is so concentrated that when the cloth is dyed, the parts covered with the paste don't take the dye, leaving the design in the original cloth color.

Example of resist printed design.

Screen Printing

This is a method of printing somewhat like stenciling. It is accomplished by using a screen, generally made of fine mesh cloth. The areas of the screen, through which the coloring passed, were filled with waterproof varnish or other insoluble filler. The color, in the form of a paste, was then forced through the untreated portions of the screen onto the fabric underneath. During World War I, screen printing took off as an industrial printing process. This process was what tablecloth manufacturers were referring to when they used the term "Hand Printed." It was mainly used at first for flags and banners but was quickly adopted for printing tablecloths from the 1920s up until approximately 1948.

Automated Screen Printing Machine

This process was thought to have been first installed by the Printex Company in California for their Vera Tablecloth line in 1946. This method advanced and automated the screen printing process, speeding up the method and allowing more creativity and flexibility for the tablecloth designer. You can identify automated screen printed tablecloths by looking for color variations in the shading. They also show a more detailed and crisper design. These tablecloths have beautiful and complex colors and designs, giving them a more three dimensional look. The floral patterns are stunning, as if you had just picked flowers from a lavish summer garden. Most of these types of tablecloths were produced after 1948.

Example of a screen printed design.

Example of an auto screen printed design, with more complex colors and shading.

Dating Tablecloths 147

Over Dying

The method in which one color is placed over another to create a third color or to add to the design is called over dying or over printing. It is usually done as a screen printing process. An example of this would be blue overprinted with yellow to make green, or red overprinted with blue to make purple. You can find many tablecloths today that demonstrate evidence of this printing style. It shows up almost as if it were a case of sloppy printing, the colors laying over each other crowding the design. Or you could say it looks as if a preschooler was given access to the printing room, creating clumsy, chunky, finger painted designs. These tablecloths were most likely produced from the late 1920s to the early 1940s.

Example of an over dyed tablecloth. First red was printed, then blue, and then green to make subtle shading.

Quick Reference Summary

Victorian: 1840-1899
- Turkey Red jacquard table covers with fringe
- Dark crimsons, maroons, browns, gold colors
- Velvets
- Felted table covers
- Rich tapestries
- Home spun textiles (uneven weaves, fringes)
- Wavy undulating stripes, "snake like designs"
- Delicate hand worked, drawn work, bobbin lace, or embroidered tablecloths

Art Nouveau: 1900
- Deep wine color
- Turkey Red damasks
- Crisp linen damasks
- Browns
- Dark cheddar yellow
- Green, purple were fugitive dyes
- Good luck symbols
- Dice
- Doves
- Hearts, ribbons, bows
- Hand worked designs

World War I: 1910s
- Colonial early Americana
- Flowers
- Long haired girls
- Stylized floral
- Oriental themes
- Pastel colors
- One directional designs
- Stamped designs, one color on linen
- Turkey Red damasks without fringe

Art Deco: 1920s
- More use of pastel colors
- No "true" greens were possible, but light sage and "Jadite Green" were possible
- Lighter color red
- Increase in number of printed colors (two or more)
- Designs are larger and usually in the corners
- Cocktail party themes
- Egyptian themes
- Aztec themes
- Oriental themes
- Damask and cotton tablecloths with colored striped borders
- Smaller sized tablecloths, 36"

The Depression: 1930s
- Home yard goods fabrics. Repeating patterns across the fabric
- Homemade feedsack tablecloths
- Small 31" squares, "breakfast cloths"
- Bright, clear, multi-color prints up to three colors
- Colors opposite the color wheel, i.e., orange/blue, orange/green, purple/yellow
- Red/white floral designs with *green* leaves. First use of true "color fast" green around 1935

- Florals with flowing ribbon designs
- Lily of the valley, cottage roses
- Larger "groupings" of florals in corners
- Large areas of grinning/shadowing around motifs
- Linen tablecloths with wide plaid edges
- Increase in "imports" from Japan, Czechoslovakia, Ireland
- "Vat Dyed," "Merchanized" terms used

World War II: 1940s
- Use of terms "Hand Printed," "Made in America," "Color Fast," "Sanforized"
- "OPA" Office of Price Administration price sticker (1942-1947)
- Florals, specially roses, dogwoods, cherry blossoms, tulips
- Tropical themes
- Berries
- Use of the term "Screen printed"
- Four+ color combinations
- 1946: Delicate shading in designs, more "realistic" three dimensional designs
- Ethnic themes: Mexican, Black Americana, Indian, Oriental
- Garden, vegetable designs
- Farm themes
- Cute children, people themes
- Western themes
- State souvenir tablecloths in larger sizes with coordinating napkins
- Coordinating dinnerware pattern tablecloths
- Hall "Autumn Leaf" (1937-1957)
- Blue Willow
- Russel Wright
- Rayon/Cotton "blends"

Prosperity: 1950s
- Continuation of 1940s designs but with richer colors and patterns
- Use of kitchen themes: dishes, bottles, spices
- Food themes
- Whimsical funny designs
- More use of bold synthetic dyes
- Metallic dyes, especially gold and silver
- Metallic threads running throughout
- Synthetic fabrics
- Rayon
- Polyester
- Black outlined designs
- "Kitschy" quirky, fun prints
- Exaggerated florals and bold geometric designs
- Modern, space age
- Heavy Danish/Swedish influence
- 1958: Tags were sewn in
- 1958: Percentage of fibers in fabrics labeled, e.g., 20% Rayon, 80% Cotton.
- Circles, squares, and other geometric shapes
- Designer "signed" tablecloths

Chapter 10
Future Collectibles

Most vintage tablecloth collectors assemble their collections with tablecloths made from the 1900s to the 1950s. The sheer number and variety of different tablecloths that can be collected from this time period is well in the thousands. But there are many wonderful, quirky tablecloths that you should consider adding to your vintage tablecloth collection as well. I like to call these "future collectibles."

Designer Signed Tablecloths

Many designers made tablecloths for their household textile collections. For example, I have several "Ralph Lauren" tablecloths that are based on vintage faded fruit designs. The famous designer, Vera, continued to make tablecloths up until the late 1980s; after approximately the 1950s, she incorporated a "ladybug" into her signature. Look for designer tablecloths with original tags and remember to remove them from the original plastic bags, storing them instead in acid-free tissue paper sold in specialty stores.

There are other signed tablecloths on the market with interesting stories to tell. One of my favorites is the "GPK" tablecloth. In 1978, Princess Grace of Monaco, looking for more artistic endeavors and freedom from royal duties, designed several patterns of sheets, towels, and tablecloths for the Springmaid Industries. These designs were based on her love of dried floral arrangements. The tablecloths were marked only "GPK" in the corner, plus a copyright of "The Springmaid Company." They were produced for only a couple of years, and of course, the beautiful Princess Grace died just a few short years later. These "GPK" tablecloths are a special treat to have in your collection.

A contemporary Ralph Lauren tablecloth capturing the elegance of the vintage 1940s fruit patterned tablecloths, 1990s. $50-$75.

Mint Grace Kelly "GPK" designed tablecloth. Manufactured by Springmaid in 1978, it's a rare, hard to find pattern. *From the William Elliott White Homestead Foundation private collection.* $150-$200.

Grace Kelly "GPK" Springmaid tag.

152 Future Collectibles

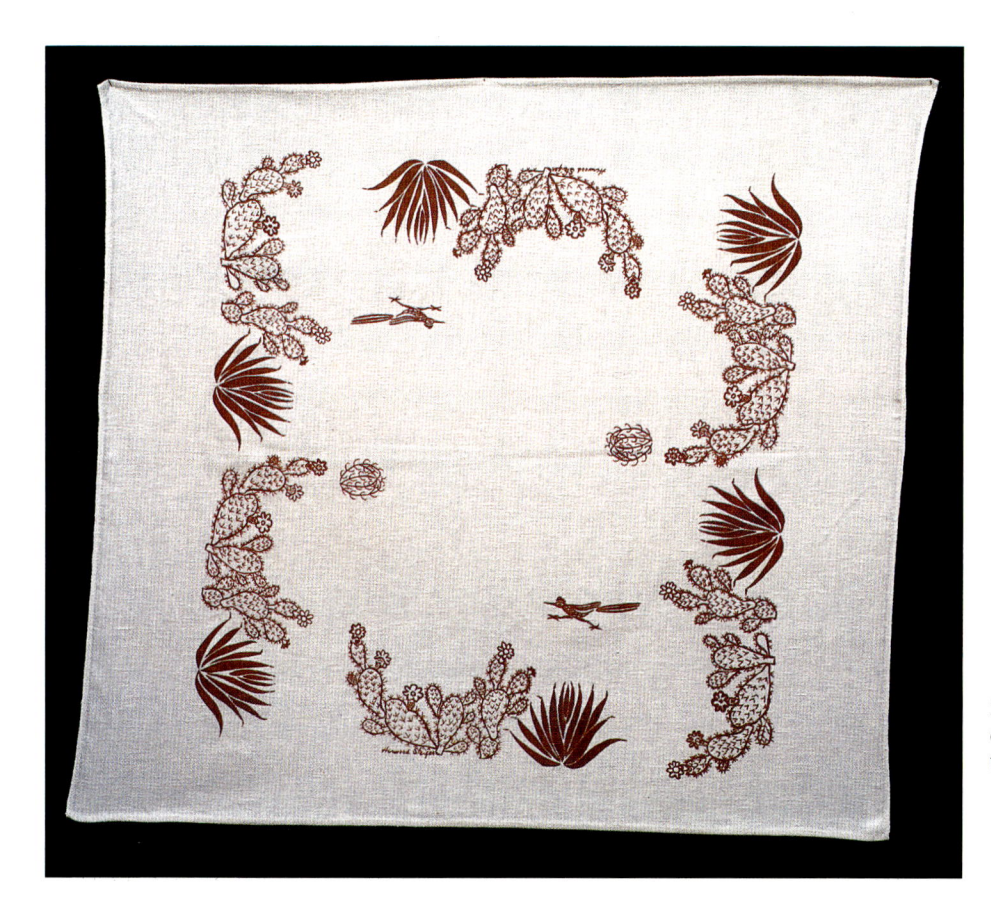

Signed "Harwood Steiger" Roadrunner designer tablecloth, early 1960s, a wonderful future collectible. $50-$75.

Themed Tablecloths

I've found a few contemporary tablecloths with unusual, limited production themes that would be delightful to add to your collection. As an example of a movie promo theme, I saw a tablecloth for the movie *Antz*, featuring a red checked gingham printed with little black ants. There are tablecloths with advertising and logo designs and even cartoon characters. I've found a "Pillsbury Doughboy" tablecloth and a "Campbell's soup kids" tablecloth. Collecting these types of tablecloths can add interest and a bit of whimsy to your collection, and will surely increase its value in the future.

Sentimental Tablecloths

I have a special tablecloth in my collection that my mother brought back from Norway last year. Hand made by local artisans in the country where my ancestors originated, it is a big heavy linen tablecloth with Viking runes stamped around the edge. It has a special place in my tablecloth collection and in my heart.

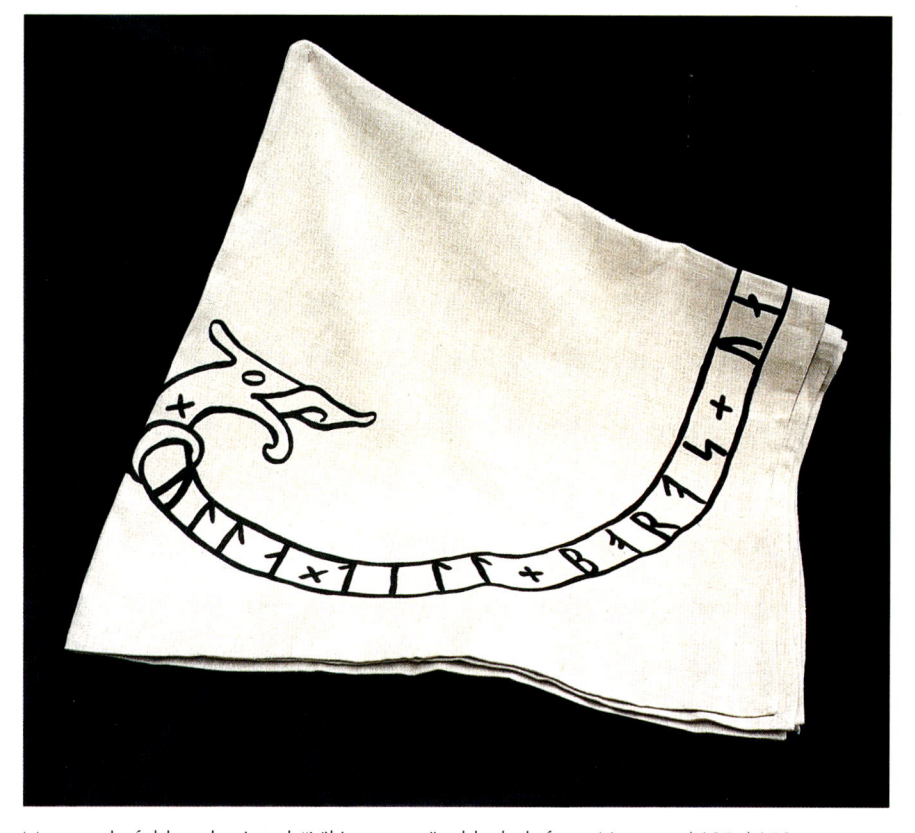

My wonderful hand printed "Viking runes" tablecloth from Norway. $125-$150.

Add tablecloths to your collection that are special to you. A hand embroidered tablecloth from a cherished grandmother, a crocheted one from your aunt, even a hand painted one from your children. You can put a note in with the tablecloth explaining its emotional value so that future generations will appreciate it as well.

Future Collectibles 153

Chapter 11
Reproductions

There are a number of reproductions of vintage tablecloths on the market today, which can be confusing for the general tablecloth collector. Most reproductions I have found either still retain the new manufacturer's tag or have been represented as "reproduction" or "vintage look" tablecloths by the dealers I have encountered. Even popular designers like Ralph Lauren have produced "vintage look" linens. There are, however, a few people that have either knowingly or unknowingly misrepresented a reproduction tablecloth as vintage. For example, I have found several people on on-line auction sites representing a reproduction "Texas" state map tablecloth as vintage and selling it for up to $80.00.

There are a few tips to keep in mind when purchasing a "vintage" tablecloth. Most vintage linens collected today were produced anywhere from 25 years to 125 years ago and will show signs of age. Even a "mint with tag" tablecloth will have areas of discoloration or slight yellowing in the fold lines. Spending a few minutes to educate yourself can save you many dollars in the future on misrepresented reproduction tablecloths.

Reproduction 1940s style "apple and berry tablecloth," 54", also comes in blue. $25-$40.

Vintage Tablecloths	Reproduction Tablecloths
Will have signs of age, discoloration	Will be crisp, new
Made from a variety of quality fabrics	Made from low grade, rough fabrics
Made with rich colorful dyes	Made with flat or dull colors

Reproduction tablecloths can be a fun way of adding that vintage look to your dining room and are sometimes easier on your wallet than the fifty-year-old originals. Since they are found in large quantities, you can have entire rooms filled with reproduction tablecloths for luncheons, parties, or even weddings. You can also rest assured that if it is stained or damaged, another one can be purchased to replace it—no more scolding your husband for spilling his glass of wine! You can find many vintage designs on the market that have been reproduced, such as "Little Mommy's Helper," "Polka Dot Fruit," and my favorite, the "Vacationland" tablecloth. Various sources for purchasing these fun reproduction linens are listed in the resource section at the back of this book.

Reproduction Florida state tablecloth/towel, 30". $14-$29.

Reproductions 155

Reproduction California State tablecloth/towel, 32". $14-$29.

Fabulous reproduction "Vacationland" tablecloth. Great 1950s style graphics and bold colors, my summer favorite. $50-$75.

This original Startex "Kitchen Parade" towel was also used as a breakfast cloth, has been reproduced, 1940s. $15-$45.

156   Reproductions

Vintage 1940s "Mommy's Little Helper" tablecloth, faded but still charming, has been reproduced. $20-$75.

Reproduction of the 1940s "Mommy's Little Helper" tablecloth, produced by Moda. The fabric is courser and thinner than the original. $25-$35.

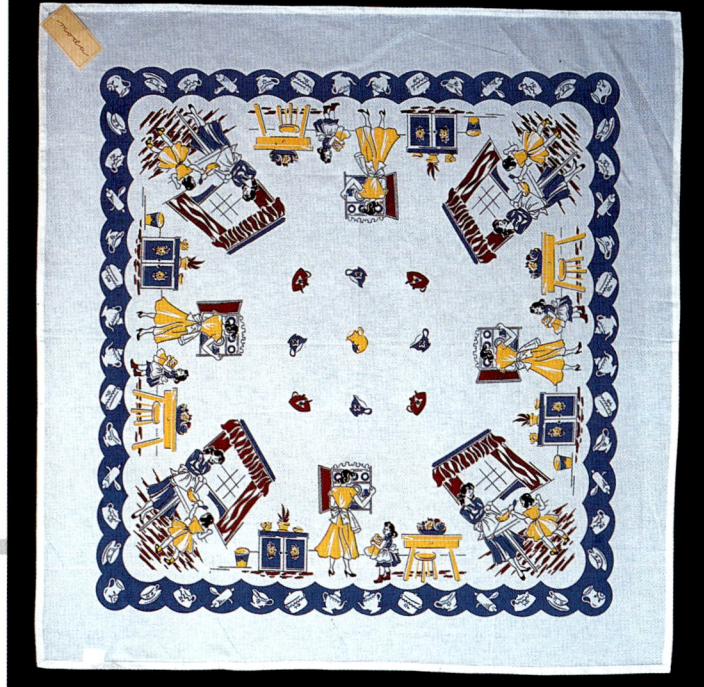

Reproduction of the Startex "Kitchen Parade" tablecloth/towel. Absence of a Startex tag and thinner cotton material are the only evidence that this is a reproduction. $14-$30.

Reproductions 157

Chapter 12

Stain Removal Guide

My best advice for a vintage tablecloth collector is not to be deterred from purchasing tablecloths with stains or small pinholes. Most yellow stains can be almost completely removed or lightened significantly by following a few simple guidelines. I enjoy displaying tablecloths with a few small holes and even those with slight stains. I believe they add character and charm to a wonderfully loved piece with a rich history. These wonderful tablecloths are anywhere from 50 to 125+ years old and were used and cherished, so they will, of course, show signs of use. Their slight imperfections are the result of years of Sunday dinners, family celebrations, and intimate dinner parties. People loved, laughed, and cried over these precious tablecloths, and I'm proud to own them.

My perfect linens are carefully stored and only brought out for "show," but my used, treasured ones with slight holes and imperfections are brought out daily and used lovingly with no fear of further damage. In fact, we add to their charm with our own little stains and rips. These "imperfect" tablecloths warm our kitchen and brighten our lives. My family is happy to cherish and use each one, knowing that each stain and imperfection is a part of its long history.

General Guidelines

First check your tablecloth to determine its approximate age (see Chapter 9). Tablecloths made prior to 1935 will have dyes that may not be colorfast and may fade or clean unevenly. Watch for any signs of the colors running out of the cloth. The water will be tinged with red, green, or orange. Remove the tablecloth immediately and rinse in cold water.

Always check your tablecloth while you are soaking or cleaning it to watch for fading colors or possible disintegration of the fabric. Here's a tip from Martha Stewart: Line your wash basin with a sheet before filling it with soap. Place larger or more fragile pieces in the basin to soak. When you are through, simply lift the material by the corners to remove it from the basin. This will help keep fragile fabrics and linens from stretching or other damage.

Do not knead, twist, or push the tablecloth too hard when removing the excess water from the tablecloth. This will further damage and rip any areas where the fabric is thin.

Here is an example of dye bleeding out. Remove immediately and rinse in cool water.

Before: A $5.00 flea market find, in bad condition, very stained. $10-$15.

After: Following the stain guidelines, this wonderful fiesta printed, textured tablecloth from the early 1940s is rescued and restored. $50-$75.

Make sure the tablecloth is free from significant wear holes that may be made larger by vigorous washing.

I have found that nature is the best bleacher. Hanging tablecloths from a clothesline or laying them outside on a sheet in the grass after washing will do a beautiful job of lightening yellow stains. Make sure that if you hang your tablecloth on the clothesline, you are not stretching the ends. Use several clothespins to hang the cloth straight across the line.

Definitions

Detergent: All-purpose synthetic detergent (liquid or powder). Use liquid detergent full strength. Mix powder with water to form a paste when working into stain.

Powdered non-chlorine bleach: Powdered bleach products such as "Biz" may be used to remove stains by soaking fabric in tepid water for length of time.

Dry-cleaning solvents: Stain and spot removers available at grocery and hardware stores. A nonflammable type is safest to use.

Stain Stick: An enzyme-based cleaner available at grocery and discount stores. Most effective on food, grease, oil, protein, and dirt-based stains and can be used on any fabric and color. Can remain on fabric for up to one week.

Out Darn Spot!

If you know what type of stain is on the cloth, the following suggestions are very helpful for removing new and sometimes older stains.

Alcoholic Drinks, Wine

Hand launder with detergent in the hottest water safe for the fabric. If it is a new stain, do not use soap (bar, flake, or detergents containing natural soap), since soap could make the stain permanent or at least much more difficult to remove.

For old stains, soak in a solution of water with one half scoop of powdered non-chlorine bleach. Watch carefully. Soak for at least two hours (more if necessary). Line dry in sun.

Soak tough stains for thirty minutes in 1 quart of warm water and 1 teaspoon of enzyme presoak product.

The removal of old or set-in stains may require washing with powdered non-chlorine bleach that is safe for the fabric. Always check for colorfastness first.

If all the sugars from the wine or alcohol are not removed, a brown stain will appear when the fabric is heated in the dryer or is ironed, as the sugar becomes caramelized in the heat.

Blood

Treat new blood stains immediately!

Flush cold water through the stain and scrape off crusted material.

Soak for fifteen minutes in a mixture of 1 quart lukewarm water, 1/2 teaspoon liquid hand dishwashing detergent, and 1 tablespoon ammonia. Use cool/lukewarm water.

Rub gently from the back to loosen stain.

Soak another for another fifteen minutes in above mixture. Rinse. Soak in an enzyme product for at least thirty minutes. Soak aged stains for several hours. Launder normally.

If the blood stain is not completely removed by this process, wet the stain with hydrogen peroxide and a few drops of ammonia. Caution: Do not leave this mixture on the cloth longer than fifteen minutes. Rinse with cool water.

If the blood stain has dried, pre-treat the area with pre-wash stain remover, liquid laundry detergent, or a paste of granular laundry product and water. Launder using bleach that is safe for the type of fabric.

Candle Wax

Harden the wax by rubbing with ice. Remove the surface wax by carefully scraping with the dull edge of a butter knife. If that does not work, you can try the next suggestion.

Sandwich the wax stain between folded paper towels and press down lightly on top of the towel with a warm (not hot) iron. Replace the paper towels frequently to absorb more wax and to prevent transferring the stain to new areas. Continue as long as wax is being removed.

Coffee, Tea

Saturate the stain with a pretreatment stain remover.

Rub the stain with a heavy-duty liquid detergent and launder in the hottest water safe for the fabric.

If it is a new stain, do not use soap (bar, flake, or detergents containing natural soap), since soap could make the stain permanent or at least more difficult to remove.

For old stains, soak the tablecloth in a solution of water with one half scoop powdered non-chlorine bleach. Watch carefully. Soak for at least two hours (more if necessary). Line dry in sun.

Dye Stains/Dye Transfer

Soak the entire tablecloth in a diluted solution of powdered non-chlorine bleach.

If the stain remains and the tablecloth is colorfast, soak the entire tablecloth in a dilute solution of liquid chlorine bleach and water. Always test for colorfastness first (see below) and watch carefully. Caution: Chlorine bleach may change the color of the tablecloth or cause irreversible damage, especially in pre-1930s tablecloths. If the stain does not come out within fifteen minutes of bleaching, it cannot be removed by this method and any further exposure to bleach will weaken the fabric and remove the color. I do not recommend this for general stain removal or for tablecloths that were made prior to 1935. Check the dating in-

Stain Removal Guide 161

formation in Chapter 9 for clues regarding the tablecloth's approximate age.

Note: To check for color fastness to liquid chlorine bleach, mix 1 tablespoon of bleach with 1/4 cup of water. Use an eyedropper to put a drop of this solution on a hidden seam in the tablecloth. Let stand two minutes, then blot dry. If there is no color change, it is probably safe to use the product. Powdered non-chorine bleaches have directions for colorfastness tests on their boxes.

There are also a number of dye removers/strippers that are available in drug and grocery stores. Be careful, however, as color removers will take out fabric colors as well as the stain.

Mildew

Mildew is a growing organism that must have warmth, darkness, and moisture to survive. Mildew actually eats cotton and linen fibers and can also attack manufactured fibers, causing permanent damage and a weakening of fibers and fabrics. It is very difficult to remove and will damage the value of a vintage tablecloth.

To treat mildew, first carefully brush or shake off the mildewed area. Pre-treat the stains by rubbing the areas with a heavy-duty liquid detergent. Then launder in the hottest water safe for the fabric, using bleach that is also safe for fabric. Remember: Always check for colorfastness and for the age of the tablecloth before using any type of bleach. Let the item dry in the sun.

Badly mildewed fabric may be damaged beyond repair. Old stains may respond to flushing with dry cleaning fluids. Carefully read and follow the instructions on the product label.

Rust

Removing rust stains can be difficult; these stains cannot be removed with normal laundering. Do not use chlorine bleach, as chlorine bleach will make the stains permanent.

Small stains may be removed with a few drops of a commercial rust remover or by repeated applications of lemon juice and salt on the stain. Do not let the fabric dry between applications.

Rinse thoroughly and launder with a liquid laundry detergent and color safe oxygen bleach or powdered non-chlorine bleach. If safe for the specific fabric, you may want to try this old home remedy: first, boil fabric in a solution of 4 teaspoons of cream of tartar per pint of water. Rinse thoroughly.

Rust removers that contain hydrofluoric acid are extremely toxic, can burn the skin, and will damage the porcelain finish on appliances and sinks. Use as a last resort.

Scorch/Burn Marks

Scorching permanently damages the fabric. The heat burns and weakens the fibers and can also melt manufactured fibers, such as polyester. If the damage is slight you may be able to improve the look. Brush the area to remove any charring.

If the tablecloth is washable, rub liquid detergent into the scorched area, then launder.

If the stain remains, bleach with an all-fabric non-chlorine bleach.

Smoke/Odors

Some older tablecloths that have been stored for many years have an "old" smell and yellowing in the creases. You will also find tablecloths that have been in a smoker's home and have that "telltale" smoke odor. I have not had any problems removing either of these odors from my tablecloths.

If the tablecloth is not seriously frayed or damaged in any other way, soak it in a solution of tepid water and one scoop of powdered non-chlorine bleach. Watch carefully for any sign of dyes fading. Remove immediately if you see green or red "tinged" water.

Soak overnight and place outside out all day in the sun. Repeat if necessary, but this should work in one treatment.

Tomato-based Stains

Saturate the area with pretreatment laundry stain remover. Wait a couple of minutes for the product to penetrate the stain. For stubborn stains, rub with heavy-duty liquid detergent. Launder immediately.

If the stain remains, soak the entire tablecloth in a diluted solution of powdered all-fabric bleach. Be aware that all the colors may lighten.

If the stain persists and the tablecloth is white or colorfast, soak in a diluted solution of liquid chlorine bleach and water. However, be sure to read the tablecloth label regarding the use of bleach. Bleach can damage some dyes and prints, and bleaching damage is irreversible. Also, if the stain is not removed in fifteen minutes, it cannot be removed by bleaching and further bleaching will only weaken the fabric.

Yellowing/Graying

For old stains, soak the tablecloth in a solution of water with one half scoop of powdered non-chlorine bleach. Watch carefully. Look for signs that the dye is colorfast. Soak for at least four hours (more if necessary). Line dry in the sun. Repeat the process if still yellow.

Chapter 13
Care and Storage of Vintage Linens

Display your vintage tablecloths in a hand painted, whitewashed cupboard.

Displaying Your Treasures

Sunlight is the vintage tablecloth's worst enemy. Exposed for long periods of time to direct sunlight, a tablecloth will fade unevenly. If you are using a tablecloth on a table that is in the sun, make sure you replace the cloth often, at least once a week.

Tablecloths look great rolled and stacked in an old open wooden "ice box" or small glass display cabinet. Draped over a whitewashed old ladder or layered on your dinner table, vintage tablecloths add charm to any home and are guaranteed to bring smiles to your guests.

If you have some of your tablecloths displayed in these ways, you might find another suggestion helpful for storing and preserving the rest of your treasures: Instead of folding the tablecloth after it is cleaned and dried, take a paper gift wrap tube and roll the tablecloth around it. Then pin in place and stack upright in a closet. This prevents fold lines, which accumulate dust and dirt and weaken the fibers. If you must fold your tablecloths, take them out occasionally, inspect them, and refold another way. If you are going to store the tablecloths in a drawer, wrap them in acid-free tissue paper (available at specialty paper stores). This will protected them from disintegrating.

In this age of new, modern designs, fast cars, and even faster computers, it is refreshing to pull out a vintage tablecloth and be transported instantly back in time, to a simpler place and era. Surrounded by luscious berries, fragrant florals, and darling whimsical designs, we can all take a moment to appreciate the "good life" of days gone by, and reflect on our own place in this fast paced, hectic world.

Layer vintage tablecloths for a "shabby chic" affect. Here, my favorite early red gingham tablecloth is paired with a small strawberry patterned tablecloth.

Restoring "Mint With Tag" Vintage Tablecloths

I am fortunate enough to have a large selection of "mint with the paper tag" vintage tablecloths. Since these treasures have been stored and unused for many years, they show signs of dirt accumulation in the fold lines. Dirt, over a period of time, will weaken the fibers and become more difficult to remove. Paper tags will also become brittle and disintegrate over time.

I wanted to use my mint tablecloths, but also retain the original tags with the tablecloths. To me, the labels are as interesting as the tablecloths themselves. They are a wonderful source of knowledge, have great graphics, and provide useful information about the manufacturers.

In order to preserve these special treasures, I carefully remove the paper label and, if it is extremely fragile, affix it to a piece of acid free cardstock. Then I use a cold small laminator (available at any craft or stationary store) to carefully laminate it with double-sided laminate. After restoring the vintage tablecloth, I attach the laminated tag to a corner of the cloth with a small gold safety pin and a pretty ribbon. I can then use the tablecloth or display it, in restored condition, along with its original tag.

Chapter 14
Creative Crafts

If a vintage tablecloth has too many holes or cannot be restored for use as a tablecloth, you can still find many other wonderful ways to enjoy your treasure. In *Terrific Tablecloths of the '40s and '50s* (Schiffer Publishing, 1998), Loretta Fehling Smith illustrates wonderful, colorful jackets and dresses that she created out of vintage linens. There is no end to creative ideas for using pieces of vintage tablecloths. Here are just a few suggestions for one-of-a-kind presents you can make for others, or for your own indulgence:

- Give your old lampshade a new look. Make a paper template to fit around the shade. Cut out your tablecloth using the template pattern, leaving a 2" edge at the top and bottom. Hot glue this material to the outside of the lampshade, then fold over the edges and glue to the back of the shade. Be sure to fold over the material on the top and bottom before gluing in place. Easy, fast, and fun.

- Cover a plain address book or photo album with a piece of vintage linen for instant nostalgia. You could also cover a diary, recipe book, or box to hold recipes.

- Tablecloths make great pillows. Add some vintage chenille and trim and you have a wonderful "cottage chic" pillow.

- Darling little girls' dresses can be made from tablecloths. Mix different patterns and textures. The vintage soft faded designs and sweet florals create one-of-a-kind priceless treasures for your little princess.

- Quilters, you already know what to do. Go for it! It would be absolutely wonderful to mix tablecloth fabric with the fabrics that are available for quilters today.

- Make a cloth doll or stuffed animal with scraps of different tablecloths.

- Cover a small corkboard with a vintage tablecloth. Add wooden details and cute push pins.

- Redecorate your garden patio with a tablecloth and matching tablecloth pillows.

- Sew up a little tablecloth tote bag for the summer.

- Make a picture frame. Glue small remnants of tablecloths around a wooden frame. Add a bow or decorative buttons for charm. These make great presents.

- Make a romantic, cottage chic wooden serving tray. Find a wooden tray at a yard sale or buy one at a craft store. Cut a piece of tablecloth to fit the inside of the tray. Using adhesive spray, carefully spray the inside of the tray, then place a piece of vintage tablecloth inside. Have a small piece of glass cut for the inside of the tray. Finish with a few small nails to hold the glass in place.

- Find a tablecloth with a simple border and plain white center. Take it to your next reunion or party and have the guests sign it with paint pens. An instant "future collectible."

- Find a plain damask or simple bordered tablecloth and on the next rainy day, have your children paint the center with colorful pictures. This makes a wonderful gift for a loved one.

Flea market lamp base repainted and shade recovered in vintage Wilendur tablecloth.

Darling pillow made from a cherry theme tablecloth.

Sweet sundress from three different vintage tablecloths.

Pair of pillows made from Wilendur red Dogwood tablecloth and vintage chenille.

Creative Crafts 167

Adorable little girl's dress made from faded vintage morning glory tablecloth.

Group of precious stuffed animals made from vintage tablecloths.

Bulletin boards covered with vintage tablecloths make great presents. Add strips of ribbon across the board to tuck pictures under.

168   Creative Crafts

Handbag made from vintage 1950s Florida souvenir tablecloth. I've seen these trendy and one-of-a-kind bags sell in boutiques for over $400.

Above right:
Matthew and Michelle's hand painted tablecloths, presents for Grandma.

Picture frames and photo album covered in vintage tablecloths.

Wooden serving trays lined with vintage tablecloths and topped with glass.

Creative Crafts 169

Chapter 15
Tablecloth Manufacturers and Their Product Lines

Here are a few of the major tablecloth manufacturers and tablecloth product lines that I have found in my research. This information can be used to date your tablecloths and to learn more about the history of vintage linens.

Abraham & Straus, 1893-1945. Produced tablecloths, doilies, towels, handkerchiefs, silk textiles.

America's Pride, 1941-1963, Weil & Durrse (Wilendure). Produced tablecloths, linens, towels, napkins.

Aristocrat, 1950-1970. Produced tablecloth and napkin sets.

Bee Figural Logo, 1916-1967. Unknown manufacturer. Produced tablecloths, tray covers, bureau scarves made of linen.

Belcrest Linens, 1945-1965, Belcrest Linens, Corp., New York. Produced tablecloths and napkin sets. From 1950 to 1965 they were imported from Hong Kong.

Broderie Creations, 1940-1965. Produced tablecloths, napkins.

Brentmoore, 1921-1941, Ely Walker Dry Goods, Missouri. Produced their own label for tablecloths and napkin sets.

Bucilla, 1919 to present.

Bur-Mil, 1940-1970, Burlington Mills Corp., North Carolina. Drapes, tablecloths, bedspreads.

Cactus Cloth, 1940-1970. Produced Souvenir tablecloth and napkin sets primarily on burlap material.

Calaprint, 1946-1968. Produced textile fabrics and table linens in California.

California Hand Prints, 1936-1969, California Hand Prints Inc. "Designed, Hand Screen Printed and Finished in Our Plant at Hermosa Beach, California." Maker of beach towels, tablecloths, clothing, and accessories.

Callaway Mills, 1932-1950. In 1889, when he was eighteen, Fuller Callaway opened Fuller Callaway's Mammoth Department Store and eventually purchased the surrounding textile mills. Fuller's sons, Carson and Fuller Callaway, Jr., assumed leadership of the mills in 1920. In 1932, they restructured and consolidated the group of textile mills into the single corporation known as Callaway Mills, Inc. They produced tablecloths, doilies, linens, and towels until 1950.

Cannon, 1916 to present, Cannon Mills, North Carolina. Produced tablecloths, napkins, drapes, pot holders. Cannon Mills company was an enterprise begun in 1906 by industrialist James William Cannon. Under the guidance of James Cannon's son, Charles, Cannon Mills came to be known as the world's largest producer of household textiles, producing sheets, towels, bedspreads, etc. They merged in 1985 with Fieldcrest Mills Inc., making Fieldcrest Cannon a world leader in household textiles. Fieldcrest Cannon was purchased by the Pillowtex Corporation in 1997 but retained the Fieldcrest Cannon name.

Charm Prints, 1939-1959, Columbus-Union Oil Cloth Company. Began by producing oilcloth tablecloths in 1929. In late 1940s, they added a line of printed tablecloths.

Crown Figural Design with words "Ely Walker," Ely Walker Dry Goods, Missouri. Produced tablecloths, napkins, carpets, handkerchiefs.

Crown Figural Design with letters GJ, 1936-1967, George Jensen Inc., New York. Produced sheets, pillowcases, tablecloths, blankets.

Davisco. 1950s label states "Originators and Distributors of originals in Novelty, Domestic Cotton Print Linens. Specialists in Barbecue Linens — Souvenir Map Luncheon Cloths, Western Design Table Coverings. This Cloth Guaranteed by the Manufacturer to Give Absolute Satisfaction. All Materials used are standard grade Osnaburg or Duck."

Dunmoy, 1953-1970, Stevens and Sons Ltd., Ireland. Produced tablecloths, napkins, glass cloths, tea cloths, tray, and cocktail cloths.

E, 1949-1961, Emporium Capwell, San Francisco, California. Produced tablecloths, table tapestries, bunting, furniture scarves.

E & W, 1906-1969, Ely Walker Dry Goods, Missouri. Produced their own line of printed tablecloths. President George Walker Bush's great-grandfather.

Edsonart, 1944, Edson Incorp., Chicago, Illinois. Card Table covers, piece goods, cotton linen, and synthetic fibers.

Everfast, 1921-1972, Everfast Fabrics, Inc., New York. Produced tablecloths, drapes, napkins, tablemats.

Favorite Things, 1950 to present. Springs Industries, Fort Mill, South Carolina. Tablecloths, runners, dish and tea towels.

Fieldcrest, 1946 - , Fieldcrest Cannon, Inc. Purchased from Marshall Fields department store, Chicago. Tablecloths, linens, and gift sets.

First Lady, 1935 to present. Mercantile Stores Company, New York. Produces tablecloths, Turkish towels, printed dish cloths.

Garden State House of Prints, 1950-1980.

Gold Label, 1961-1981, Cannon Mills Corp., North Carolina. Tablecloths, coverlets, napkins.

Gold Medal Brand, 1893-1949, William Liddell, Co., Chicago, London, Dublin. Produced tablecloths, tray cloths, damasks, tea cloths, supper cloths, sideboard cloths, basin cloths.

Gribbons, Styled by Gribbons, 1923-1968, Gribbon Company, New York. Plain and embroidered linen and damask tablecloths.

Gumps, 1939-1968, S & G Gump Company, California. Produced tablecloths, napkins, placemats, drapes.

Hadon, 1945-1970, Haddad & Sons Inc., New York. Produced tablecloths, scarves, and clothing.

Happy Home, 1957-1976, F.W. Woolworths, New York. Produced tablecloths and curtains.

Hard-o-craft, 1950 to present. James Hardy & Co. Produced tablecloths, napkins, table runners, doilies, placemats.

Hardy Tex, 1939, James G. Hardy & Co. Produced tablecloths, napkins, table runners, doilies, placemats.

Hardycraft, 1923 to present. James G. Hardy & Co., Inc. Produced tablecloth and napkin sets, towels, and other kitchen textiles.

G. Hardy & Company, 1923 to present. Supplier of hotel and restaurant linens.

Harmony House. Sears' own label produced tablecloths and other household goods from 1940 to 1960.

Harwood Steiger Inc., 1956 to present. Harwood Steiger was a prominent western fabric designer from 1956 until his death in 1980. He created hand printed, silk-screened fabrics, suitable for clothing, draperies, wall hangings, etc. He also sold linen dish towels, tablecloths, and placemats. Steiger's sister-in-law still sells his wonderful designs in a small shop in Arizona.

Hawaiiprint, 1963 to present, Hawaii Print Corp., Hawaii. Bed linens, tablecloth sets made from woven and knit fabrics

Heirloom, 1950-1970, Bates Manufacturing Company, Maine. Known for their great 1950s bedspreads, they also produced tablecloths and napkins.

Indian Head Mills, founded in 1835 in Boston, Massachusetts. In 1898, the mill was moved to South Carolina. In the 1900 census, the town's population was shown as 567. Due to the success of the mill, the population rose in 1910 to 1,747. The cotton mill closed in 1963.

Lancaster Cotton Mills, 1895-1914. Lancaster Prints, Springs Industries 1914 to present. Leroy Springs established the mill in Lancaster, South Carolina.

Leacock Quality Prints, 1950-1969, New York. Produced tablecloths, napkins.

Leda, 1951-1971, Leda Lee Design, California. Produced tablecloths and other kitchen textiles.

Martex, 1930 to present, WestPoint Stevens Inc., South Carolina. One of the oldest textile mills in the South, this company is currently made up of three textile giants from the past. J.P Stevens is the company's oldest name, dating back to 1813. Pepperell Manufacturing Company Inc. was founded in 1851 in Biddeford, Maine. Incorporated in 1880, West Point Manufacturing Company was based in West Point, Georgia. In 1965, West Point and Pepperell merged. Stevens was acquired in 1988.

Maytex, 1944-1990, Maytex Mills, Inc., New York. Produced house wares, tablecloths, placemats, kitchen towels.

ML Cloth, 1950-1970. Produced tablecloths and napkins.

Mosse, 1916-1965, Mosse Inc. Produced tablecloths, linens, blankets for the yachting industry.

Nileen, 1947-1968, Simtex Mills, New York. Produced tablecloths, napkins.

Parisian Prints, 1960 - present. Produced tablecloths, souvenir tablecloths.

Pennicraft, 1946-1975. J.C. Penney's own label of tablecloths and other kitchen textiles.

Pine Tree Linens, 1927-1947. Produced tablecloths, luncheon sets, doilies, card table sets, breakfast sets, dinner sets.

Pride Of Flanders, 1930-1970 Specialized in "Irish Linens."

Prints Charming, 1963-1985, Sun Weave Linen Corp., New York. Produced tablecloths, napkins, linens.

Printex, 1936 to present. Company founded in 1936 by Vera and her husband to produce "Vera" line and other "art" linens.

Prismacolor G&W, 1970-1985 (spinning wheel logo). Produced tablecloths and towels.

Rosemary, 1922 to present, Rosemary Manufacturing, New York. Produced table linens, damasks, jacquard woven fabrics. Purchased by J.P Stephens in the 1980s.

Royal Household, 1906-1969, Cannon Mills Co., Inc. Produced tablecloths, napkins, and bedspreads.

Setting Pretty, 1944-1962. Weil & Durrse, Inc. (Wilendure), New York, produced this line of tablecloths, napkins, placemats, towels, cotton pieces.

Simtex, 1946-1968, a division of Simmons Co., 40 Worth Street, New York. Produced tablecloths, bedspreads, upholstery, and plain piece goods. Purchased by J.P. Stevens in the 1960s.

Springmaid, 1887 to present. Springs Industries was founded in 1887 as Fort Mill Manufacturing Company in Fort Mill, South Carolina, by Samuel Elliott White. In 1919, Spring Maid cotton mills operated five textile mills in South Carolina as separate companies: Fort Mill Plant, White Plant, Lancaster Plant, Kershaw Plant, and Eureka Plant. In 1933, all the plants were incorporated into The Springs Cotton Mills. In 1947, they began producing tablecloths and napkins along with their household textile products. Now known as Spring Industries.

Stalwart, 1947-1970, R.H Macy Co., New York. Produced tablecloths, sheets, pillowcases. Used Indian Head Cotton.

Startex (with "star" incorporated into design), 1920-1945; Startex (without "star"), 1945-2001, Startex Mills, South Carolina. Printed tablecloths, kitchen towels. Purchased by Reigel Textile Corp in the 1960s. Now owned by the Clifton Manufacturing Company.

State Pride, 1954 to present, Belk Stores Services Inc., North Carolina. Produces tablecloths, aprons, bedspreads, drapes, coverlets, towels.

STC (Standard Textile Company), 1942-1979, Standard Textile Co., Ohio. Produced tablecloths, sheets, toweling, huck towels.

Tanvald, 1921-1967, Hermann & Jacobs Corp., New York. Produced tablecloths and napkins from fine linen and cotton.

The Emporium, 1896-1949, San Francisco, California. Emporium Capwell produced tablecloths, table tapestries, bunting, furniture scarves.

The Linen Of Queens, 1948-1975, D. Porthoult Inc., New York. Household linens, tablecloths, napkins.

Thomas Gold Label Print, 1950 to present. Produced tablecloths and napkins.

Thomaston, 1927 to present, Thomaston Cotton Mills, Georgia. Produced cotton and damask tablecloths and napkins.

Thomaston Mills, 1899 to present, Thomaston, Georgia. In 1899, a group of local investors led by Robert E. Hightower, whose family had been in Georgia since before the American Revolution, chartered Thomaston Cotton Mills. There was cotton in abundance and access to railroads. By the 1950s, the company employed the best textile stylist in the industry (according to a corporate history) and went after the discount market just as colored home textiles were coming into vogue.

Vera, 1935 to present, Vera Inc., Los Angeles, California. Produced tablecloths, napkins, scarves, and clothing.

Vicray, 1946-1966, Kemp & Beatley, New York. Produced tablecloth sets.

Victory, 1919-1940, Kemp & Beatley, New York. Produced tablecloths, doilies, and table covers.

Victory (figural crown), K & B, 1919-1972, Kemp & Beatley, New York. Tablecloth protectors, pads.

Wifitex. 1950s tablecloth manufacturer.

Wilendur, 1939-1958, Weil & Durrse, New York. Produced tablecloths, napkins, placemats, runners.

Wilendure, 1958-1990, Weil & Durrse, New York. Produced tablecloths, napkins, placemats, runners.

Yucca Prints, 1930 to present, Barth & Dreyfuss, Los Angeles, California. Produced souvenir and "Western" style tablecloths and napkin sets from 1930 to 1960. Still produces products for home furnishings. Barth & Dreyfuss of California designs, manufactures, and distributes high quality kitchen and bath decor.

Label showing list of coordinating items available for Bucilla "Folklore." available label.

Callaway tag.

ML Cloths tag.

California Hand Prints tag.

Gribbon Pure Linens tag.

Prints Charming E/S tag.

Vicray K&B tag.

Queen Anne Indian Head Cloth tag.

Back of "Prints Charming E/S" tag, explaining their chromatic dye method.

Springmaid "St Regis" Lancaster tag.

Tablecloth Manufacturers, 1840-1960

Chapter 16

Useful Resources

On-line Stores

There are a vast number of vintage tablecloth and linen dealers on the web. Just typing in "vintage linens" or "vintage tablecloths" in your search engine will give you hours and hours of shopping pleasure from the comfort of your own computer. Here are a few of my favorite on-line dealers, and of course, you can buy vintage linens and tablecloths on almost all of the popular "on-line auction sites" as well.

Easy Street Antiques
www.easystreetantiques.com
Vintage textiles, including tablecloths, runners, towels, hankies, lace, fabric, and scarves.

Sharon's Antiques Vintage Fabrics
www.rickrack.com
610-756-6048
Inventory includes vintage and antique cotton fabrics, feedsacks, quilts, and quilt blocks; also kitchen towels, aprons, hankies and vintage printed tablecloths.

Reprodepot Fabrics
www.reprodepotfabrics.com
206-938-5585
They specialize in vintage reproduction fabrics, tablecloths, trimmings, house wares, and gifts. Their products have been featured on HGTV's *Smart Design* program, *Country Living* and *Parents* magazines, and *Better Homes and Gardens* special interest publications.

Vintage Linen Warehouse
www.vintagelinen.com
They have been in linen business for over fifteen years and sell a nice selection of vintage linens and tablecloths.

Textile Museums

Several textile mill museums are dedicated to preserving and interpreting the history and heritage of the American textile industry. Most of them have on-line web sites and virtual "galleries" were you can learn more about the mills, their employees, and their history. Below are a few of the museums that specialize in vintage textiles; they are a wonderful source for additional information.

The Textile Museum
2320 S Street, NW
Washington, DC 20008-4088
202-667-0441

The American Textile History Museum
491 Dutton Street
Lowell, Massachusetts 01854-4221
978-441-0400

The Mill Museum
157 Union Street
Willimantic, Connecticut 06226
860-456-2178
www.millmuseum.org

The Charles River Museum of Industry
154 Moody Street
Waltham, Massachusetts 02453
781-893-5410
www.crmi.org

The Windham Textile & History Museum
157 Union/Main Streets
Willimantic, Connecticut 06226
860-456-2178

Boott Cotton Mills Museum
400 Foot of John Street
Lowell, Massachusetts 01852
978-970-5000
www.nps.gov/lowe/loweweb/Lowe%20exhibits.htm

Glossary

Aniline Dyes. Chemical dyes (as opposed to vegetable ones) derived from coal tar. These were developed for use in the late 1850s.

Crash. A linen cotton or cotton mix suitable for kitchen towels. Better grades with softer feel and higher thread counts are used for tablecloths.

Damask. A fabric of silk, rayon, and cotton or other combinations of fibers woven in jacquard weave with reversible flat designs.

Dry Goods. An early marketing term for textile fabrics.

Dyestuff. Dyes used for printing color on textiles.

Embroidery. Ornamental needlework done on the fabric itself.

Fugitive. An unstable dye that tends to run, fade, or change colors.

Ghost Fabric. A textile that contained a fugitive dye, leaving no color or only a little color. This condition is most often seen in some red and green dyes as well as pinks and blues from the 1850s to the 1930s.

Homespun. A very coarse, rough linen, wool, or cotton or man-made fiber or blend in varied colors, generally in a plain weave.

Linen. This is the strongest of the vegetable fibers and has two to three times the strength of cotton. It is made from flax, a bast fiber taken from the stalk of the plant. Its luster comes from the natural wax content. Creamy white to light tan, this fiber can be easily dyed and the color does not fade when washed. Linen does wrinkle easily.

Madder. A shrubby herb grown for the dyeing properties of its root. Madder is the basic colorant for Turkey Red and the coppery browns of the late 1800s.

Mercerization. A process originally developed by John Mercer about 1850, mercerization was forgotten until 1890 when the idea was patented. It is a process that gives an increase in flexibility, strength, and luster to cotton tablecloths. It was advertised on tablecloths produced between 1920 and 1940.

Mordant. A chemical agent that fixes a dyestuff to a fiber.

Over Dyed/Over Printed. A tablecloth that was vat dyed in two different baths, or stamped first with one color then stamped or overprinted with another to create a third color.

Plush. A heavy-pile fabric with a deeper pile than velvet or velour.

Rayon. Made from cellulose, rayon has many of the qualities of cotton, a natural cellulose fiber. Rayon is strong, extremely absorbent, comes in a variety of qualities and weights, and can be made to resemble natural fabrics. Rayon does not melt but burns at high temperatures. Kenneth Lord, Sr., coined the word "rayon" in 1924 during an industry sponsored contest to find a name for what was then known as "artificial silk."

Sailcloth. A generic name for fabrics that are used for sails. Sailcloth is usually made of cotton, linen, jute, or nylon and is a heavy, almost canvas-like fabric. It was a favorite fabric of both Wilendur and Startex.

Sanforized. Trade name of a process for shrinkage control, meaning residual shrinkage of not over 1% guaranteed. It was developed in the 1950s and advertised on some tablecloth tags during that time.

Tapestry. A jacquard woven fabric in cotton, wool, or man-made fibers. The design is woven in by means of colored filling yarns. On the back, shaded stripes identify this fabric.

Turkey Red. A specific shade of red produced from the madder plant. The technique involved placing fabric in an oil bath. A colorfast dye, it was first developed in Turkey. Turkey Red can fade to pink with use.

Velour. A smooth, closely woven pile fabric usually of cotton, wool, or man-made fibers. It is heavier than velvet.

Velvet. Silk, rayon, nylon or acrylic cut pile fabric.

Bibliography

Adams, Sara Swain. *How to set the table for any occasion*. New York, New York: Derryvale Linen Co., Inc., 1918.

Bosker, Gideon, and Michele Mancici. *Fabulous Fabrics of the 50's*. San Francisco, California: Chronicle Books, 1992.

Carmichael, W.L., George E. Linton, and Isaac Price. *Callaway Textile Dictionary*. La Grange, Georgia: Callaway Mills, 1947.

Dolan, Maryanne. *Old Lace & Linens, Including Crochet*. Alabama: Books Americana, 1989

Johnson, George H. *Textile Fabrics*. New York, New York: Harper & Brothers, 1927.

Johnston, Meda Parker, and G. Kaufman. *Design on Fabrics*. New York, New York: Van Nostrand Reinhold Company, 1967.

Lewis, Dora S., Gladys Citek Peckham, and Helen Stone Hovey. *Family Meals and Hospitality*. New York, New York: The MacMillan Company, 1953.

Kurella, Elizabeth. *The Complete Guide to Vintage Textiles*. Iola, Wisconsin: Krause Publications, 1999.

Meller, Susan, and Joost Elffers. *Textile Designs*. New York, New York: Harry N. Abrams, Inc., 1991.

Pettus, Lousie. *The Springs Story, Our First Hundred Years*. South Carolina: Springs Industries, Inc., 1987.

Smith, Loretta Fehling. *Terrific Tablecloths from the '40s & '50s*. Atglen, Pennsylvania: Schiffer Publishing Ltd., 1998.

Smith, Georgiana R. *Table Decoration Yesterday, Today & Tomorrow*. Vermont: Charles E. Tuttle Company, 1968.

Wilson, Kax. *A History of Textiles*. Boulder, Colorado: Westview Press, Inc., 1979.

Wingate, Isabel. *Textile Fabrics and Their Selection*. New York, New York: Prentice-Hall, 1949.